THE
REDEVELOPMENT
GUIDE

Dr. Adv. Harshul Savla
Adv. Darsh Dharod

INDIA · SINGAPORE · MALAYSIA

ISBN
Paperback 979-8-89588-355-6
Hardcase 979-8-89610-977-8

About the Author

Dr. Adv. Harshul Savla (MRICS)

Dr. Adv. Harshul Savla (MRICS) is Managing Partner of M Realty (Suvidha Lifespaces) which has successfully completed more than 2 million sq.ft. in last 35 years across Mumbai City under the able leadership of Mr. Pramesh Rambhiya. CRISIL India and Realty Icon Awards recognized Dr. Harshul as "Young Thought Leader" and Realty NXT featured him as "Young Turk of Real Estate Sector". He has won the prestigious CREDAI-MCHI Golden Pillar Award in the category of Best Debutant Real Estate Developer and has been awarded "Young Achiever of the Year" by ET NOW, CNN News 18, ZEE Business, MAHARASHTRA Times, ABP News, Realty+, MID DAY, Business World and Realty Quarter.

Dr. Harshul has featured in the Business World and Realty Plus "40 under 40" list as Real Estate's Young Turk consecutively in 2021, 2022, 2023 and 2024. He has also been awarded the prestigious "Pillars of Maharashtra" award in 2022 by Hon'ble Member of Parliament for Mumbai North. The Times Group's Economic Times has awarded Dr. Harshul Savla as an Inspiring Personality 2022 for exceptional contribution to Real Estate Sector. Mid Day's "Success Stories 2022" has featured Dr. Harshul's various achievements and journey. He has been a TEDx Speaker too.

Dr. Harshul has worked as EA to Ramesh Nair, former Chairman, JLL India and has worked in the Wealth Management Team at TATA Capital where he was awarded the National Award for Exemplary Performance. He is a perfect blend of Corporate Experience along with stellar education credentials of Ph.D., LL.M, LL.B, MBA and BMS from prestigious institutions like JBIMS, GLC, NM and Department of Law, University of Mumbai.

Dr. Harshul holds the World Record for "Maximum Degree from Single University" and his World Record is mentioned in World Book of Records London, The British World Records, International Book of Records, International Talent Book of Records, Exclusive World Record, Asian World Records, Global Records & Research Foundation, Amazing Indian Records, World Records India, India Book of Records, Kohinoor Vidyasamrat, Champion Book of World Record, High Range Book of World Records etc.

He also holds the World Record for "Maximum Books Authored & Published in a Year" for authoring and publishing 12 Real Estate Books in the year 2021 in English Language. Dr. Harshul is awarded as "Author of the Year" at the prestigious CNBC Awaaz Real Estate Excellence Awards 2022 held at Taj Lands End, Mumbai.

Dr. Harshul was awarded Doctorate (Ph.D.) for his Thesis on REITs (Real Estate Investment Trusts) which is first such thesis in India on the said subject and the Thesis is also available in the form of a book. Apart from this he is an NSE Certified Market Professional - Level 4 and has done a course on 'Strategic Real Estate Management' from ISB, Hyderabad.

Dr. Harshul is "Chairman: Statistics & Standards" at CREDAI National, which has more than 13,300 Real Estate Developers as its Members and has presence in 230 Cities (21 State Chapters). He is Research Convenor of CREDAI MCHI and heads its Statistics & Research Wing. CREDAI MCHI is a leading Real Estate Developers Association of MMR having 1,800 members across its 14 Units. Dr. Harshul has also served as the National Head of the Committee on E-Learning and Masterclass at CREDAI National Youth Wing from 2021-2023 and is presently the "Chairman: Business Process Optimization"

Dr. Harshul is also an Amazon Best Selling Author and has authored 22 books on the Real Estate Sector and General Management, making his books one of India's most comprehensive literatures on Real Estate Sector. Some of his books are: Real Estate Laws, Reality of Realty, Real Estate Valuation, Affordable Housing, NBFC & HFC Crisis, Fractional Ownership & REITs, Insolvency & Bankruptcy Code, Self-Redevelopment & Reviving Stalled Projects, Digitalizing Real Estate Sector in Built Environment, Building Information Modeling, Green Buildings, Facility Management, COVID-O-NOMICS, Luxury Retail, Alternative Real Estate, Judicial Journey under RERA, Self-Redevelopment and Reviving Stalled Projects, NCLT & IBC in Real Estate Sector, ERA POST RERA, Funding Options for Developers, FSI – A Development Control Tool, The Redevelopment Guide, MAHA RERA etc. He regularly writes articles for fortnightly business magazine "Property House" and may other newspapers and journals.

Dr. Harshul is Associate Professor at ITM University and is also a Ph.D. Guide / Supervisor with them. He was a Visiting Faculty and Guest Lecturer at the prestigious RICS School of Built Environment, Mumbai Campus. He taught the subject 'Real Estate Development Process' to Management Students at the Mumbai Campus. He was also a Guest Lecturer at REMI - The Real Estate Management Institute, Mumbai. He was Invited to conduct Session on REITs in India for Developers Members of NAREDCO and was one of the youngest Member Developer to do so. He has also delivered a lecture at PEATA (I) on Future of Realty. He is also a renowned moderator for panels discussing various aspects of Realty and has moderated more than 60 panel discussions so far.

Dr. Harshul has recently embarked his research journey for his second Ph.D. which he is pursuing from the Department of Law, University of Mumbai under the guidance of Former HOD of the Department. His thesis is on the topic of RERA and will be the first Ph.D. in Law thesis in India on RERA.

Dr. Harshul is also the Founding Member of the "RERA Practitioners' Welfare Association" and the Founding Member of "IRIYA Realty Intelligentsia and Advisory Foundation of India" which comprises of Innovation Centre, Think Tank and Centre of Excellence. Dr. Harshul is also part of the Managing Committee of IBG (India Business Group). Dr. Harshul is a Founding Member at the 500 MBA Club and also a Mentor at the Founder Institute which is the world's most proven network to turn ideas into fundable startups and startups into global businesses.

About the Author

Adv. Darsh Rekha Ketan Dharod

Adv. Darsh Rekha Ketan Dharod is a young millennial of 27 years having keen interest and plethora of knowledge about the Real Estate Industry.

Adv. Darsh has been keenly watching and tracking the real estate industry from about when he was in his pre-teens, the spark and interest kicked-off in him while visiting a few under construction projects and subsequent interactions with key stakeholders and stalwarts from the industry.

Adv. Darsh is an alumnus of Bombay Scottish School, Mahim an institution which is 177 years old, ranked among the top 2 in Mumbai and top 6 in India. He stood among the top 1 percent in the ICSE Board 10th Grade examinations.

Adv. Darsh has degrees in Accountancy, Finance, Management and Law having studied Bachelors of Accountancy and Finance (B.A.F) from H.R. College of Commerce and Economics in which he stood at 6th Rank in entire University of Mumbai, Bachelors of Law (LL.B) from K.C. Law College, Masters of Commerce in Management (M.Com) and Masters of Law (LL.M) from University of Mumbai and is currently in the last and final stage of completing Chartered Accountancy (CA) from Institute of Chartered Accountants of India and Chartered Financial Analyst (CFA) from CFA Institute, USA.

Adv. Darsh started working rather at an early age of 19 years while still in college, managing both studies and work which has helped him work in different industries.

Adv. Darsh as part of Chartered Accountancy course has completed 3 years of articleship, there after worked in Tata Capital, a Tata Group Company in Special Projects developing a new digitally enabled platform driving collaboration among its business enabling the dream of 'One Tata' which eventually took the shape as the super app 'Tata Neu'. He later worked at HDFC Property Ventures a Real Estate Private Equity Fund and a HDFC Group Company and IEG Investment Banking Group, a German based Investment Bank. He has also worked at Colliers International in their Consulting and Advisory team, in which he advised on various Real Estate Developments and Asset classes to top Developers,

Industrialists and Governments in 25 cities across 7 States and 2 UTs in India.

In his stint at Adani Realty, in CEOs Office- Strategic Projects, he was part of the founding member team for Dharavi Redevelopment Project which is Asia's Largest Slum Rehabilitation and Urban Regeneration Project. Currently, in Godrej Properties, he is a part of the Business Development, Investments and Acquisition team, responsible for acquiring new greenfield and brownfield projects for Godrej Properties in form of Land acquisitions, Strategic investments and Redevelopment opportunities.

Adv. Darsh has been recipient of many prestigious awards in his life such as the "R.K. Sharma Memorial Prize" for highest distinction in ICSE Examinations, Letter of Appreciation from Mr. Rajendra Darda, Editor-in-chief Lokmat and Minister of School Education in Government of Maharashtra. He was felicitated with various awards during his college years for his contribution to college and academic performance by Dr. Indu Shahani, Principal of H.R. College of Commerce and Economics and former Sheriff of Mumbai. He's also been recipient of awards by Bombay Scottish School, K.C. Law College, KVO, LNMA among many others.

Adv. Darsh is actively involved and one of the youngest committee members in the history of CREDAI MCHI (Confederation of Real Estate Developers' Association of India & Maharashtra Chamber of Housing Industry), where he is a part of Statistics and Research Wing. CREDAI MCHI has more than 1800 Developers as its members across 14 City Chapters making up for entire Mumbai Metropolitan Region.

Adv. Darsh is also actively involved and is also one of the youngest committee members in the history of CREDAI National Youth Wing, where he is a part of Business Process Automation Committee. CREDAI National has more than 13,300 Developers as its members in 21 States and 230 City Chapters across India.

Adv. Darsh is also an Amazon Best Selling Author and has authored more than 8 books on the Real Estate Sector, making his books one of India's most comprehensive literatures on Real Estate Sector. Some of his books are: Self-Redevelopment & Reviving Stalled Projects, Alternative Real Estate, Insolvency & Bankruptcy Code, Judicial Journey under RERA, ERA post RERA, Funding Options for Developers, FSI- A Development Control Tool, The Redevelopment Guide etc.

Adv. Darsh due to his rich and diversified academic and professional experience, regularly holds Seminars and is also a Guest Lecturer on different topics covering Finance, Law, Real Estate, among others at prestigious colleges in India. He has also written articles and snippets for a few newspapers, magazines and journals.

Adv. Darsh has mentored over 50 students pursuing their Masters, MBA and other specialization courses from institutions and universities such as NMIMS, IIT- Kharagpur, CEPT, NICMAR, RICS, GLC, MIT, UC Berkley, Cranfield, HSNC, Nirma, KC law, Amity among others. Adv. Darsh has also been the guide for final year Dissertation, Thesis, DRP for many of the above students.

Adv. Darsh is also actively involved in a few NGOs and for his contributions to society has been facilitated by Ministry of Railways, Government of India among many other organizations. He has also represented India at an UNESCO event held in Europe and Turkey.

Adv. Darsh has keen interest in sports, has run several marathons and been a gold medalist in Swimming, Chess and Badminton.

NATIONAL BEST SELLING REAL ESTATE SERIES

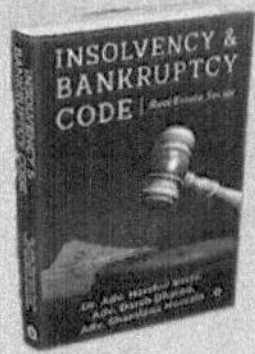

Contents

Contents

Section A

Redevelopment

Chapter 1

History of Real Estate development

Real Estate has evolved over the past century all across the Indian Subcontinent.

The rapid pace of real estate development in Mumbai over the last century is unmatched or unseen anywhere in India.

The Origins:

Mumbai was a group of seven islands gifted to King Charles II of England in 1661 by the King of Portugal as a marriage gift. Later the seven islands were merged together to form Mumbai, then known as "Bombay" For a few centuries up until the independence, Mumbai has been a predominantly a port city and hub for trade and commerce.

Even though "The Saraswat Cooperative Housing Society" was Asia's first such Cooperative Housing Society, which came into being in 1915 in Mumbai, it wasn't until the 1960s that the trend of Cooperative Housing Societies picked up pace in the City of Mumbai.

Real estate activity in Mumbai gained pace in the 1960s with the development of many cooperative housing societies across the region. This was fueled in one part by the legal framework around CHS being laid down clearly under the Maharashtra Co-operative Housing Societies Act, 1960. Other reasons for the growth and adoption of CHS were:-

- Formation of a separate states of Maharashtra and Gujarat, with Mumbai being Maharashtra's Capital

- Financial Institutions (Mainly Banks) and LIC giving out loans of as much as 80% to individuals or, in most cases, group of individuals who were mainly their employees and who undertook such development by having own contribution of 20%

The real estate sector boomed and saw hyper growth during about 20 years between 1960s to 1980s when more than 10,000 Co-operative Housing Societies were developed and registered across Mumbai (then known as Bombay) and its extended suburbs (Now the entire area is known as Mumbai Metropolitan Region)

Figure 1: Mumbai in its early days

From the 1980s onwards, Mumbai (then Bombay) started seeing advent of builder led real estate development as the funding to these individuals or group of individuals who were self developing properties started drying up. Also around the same time the entire ecosystem started developing around developers, contractors and certain financial institution, which further increased the pace of builder led development in the city of Mumbai

Through the 1980s, 1990s and 2000s saw huge land parcels being developed even outside the island city of Mumbai, across the Mumbai Metropolitan Region. Areas in Powai, Andheri, Thane, Mira-Bhayander, Navi-Mumbai started seeing a lot of Real estate activity, projects on a large scale and diversified real estate asset classes also started coming up

As such, during these decades Mumbai grew across its length and breadth, horizontally and also vertically. But as Mumbai grew over these decades, land parcels across the city started getting exhausted, with very few land parcels of good real estate development potential with good demand capability left across the region. Hence Redevelopment is one of the main ways in which Mumbai has been getting developed for a good portion of this century and this is the only plausible way Mumbai can further grow over the coming decades.

Over the years, many laws have been enacted and implemented for the development of Mumbai City and its Suburbs (MMR), which have helped and also fueled the development potential and the demand that the city has seen.

Figure 2: Mumbai in 21st Century

Social housing and land relationships

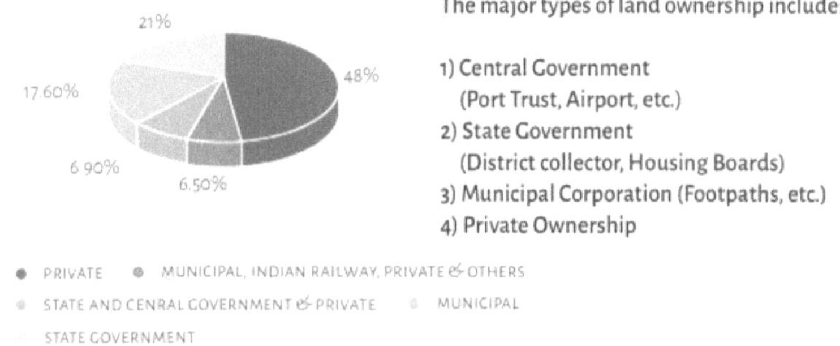

Figure 3: Mumbai Land Ownership

Some of the Marquee laws are:-

1. Bombay Town Planning Act, 1915

2. Maharashtra Co-operative Housing Societies Act, 1960

3. Maharashtra Ownership of Flat Act, 1963

4. Maharashtra Regional Town Planning Act, 1966

5. Maharashtra Slum Areas (Improvement, Clearance And Redevelopment) Act, 1971

6. Urban Land (Ceiling and Regulation) Act, 1976

7. Coastal Regulation Zone Rules 1991

8. Securitisation and Reconstruction of Financial Assets and Enforcement of Security Interest Act, 2002

9. Land Acquisition Rehabilitation and Resettlement Act, 2013

10. Insolvency and Bankruptcy Code, 2016

11. Real Estate (Regulation and Development) Act, 2016

12. Development Control & Promotion Regulation, 2034

Chapter 2

Concept of Redevelopment

Redevelopment essentially means when one demolishes an existing old property, improvises it and constructs a new property on the same land space. Basically, one look at a property, vacant or existing and seeing how to improve upon it, giving it a better aesthetics, making best and optimum use of the space available to provide good living experience to the ultimate residents who make this space their home. Redevelopment is done to add value and increase the life of the property. The prime advantage of such transformation is the usual difference between the old and the new property.

Usage of a better quality of materials in the redevelopment will assure the society members that they will not face any significant structural or maintenance related issues for the next 15 to 20 years. The redevelopment process can be a challenging task unless the developer gets full cooperation from society. On the other hand, the developer should keep transparency about any decisions or changes that would take place in the redevelopment process.

Figure 4: Ongoing Redevelopment Project

Advantages of Redevelopment

To Society Members:

- Additional Area:

  An additional area is provided to the members of society in the process of redevelopment. An Architect or a Project Management Consultant (PMC) prepares a feasibility report in which it is discussed how much additional area will be provided to society's respective members. Apart from getting additional area free of cost, the members get a chance to buy extra area within the same flat that is being provided to them at a discounted price.

Figure 5: Redeveloped Building providing bigger areas

- Newer Building:

  Rainwater harvesting, green buildings, solar heating and fire alarm systems are provided in the redeveloped building. New parking facilities are also offered in the redeveloped buildings. The newly developed property provides earthquake-resistant structure, better planned and designed flats, modern elevators, wider staircase, and passages as per DCPR.

Figure 6: Newer and Modern Buildings

- Amenities:

  In a new development, many modern amenities are made available like podium, clubhouses, gardens, children's play area, swimming pool, gymnasium, community hall, etc.

Figure 7: Club House and other Amenities

- Car parking:

  New buildings provide ample parking space as well, in old buildings and developments there are limited parking spaces, in new buildings every flat has parking, this leads to less congestion on roads where most of the cars are still parked in the city.

Figure 8: Dedicated and bigger parking areas

To Developers:

- Asset Light Model:

  The developer would carry a low amount of initial investment as he does not have to invest capital in purchasing the land. The developer saves money in clearing some approvals as the land title of the proposed property is clean and clear.

- Better Cash Flow Management:

  Positive cash flows are critical for any business; redevelopment helps in getting cash flows in the business so that the revenue from the sale of flats is matched with the cost of construction.

- Brand Presence:

  The developer gets an opportunity to present its brand value in the market and gain loyal customers, which can be beneficial in the future.

- Infrastructure in place:

  The developer has to pay the negligible cost of infrastructure as most of it already exists. Examples include main approach roads, water supply, sewerage and electric supply.

Figure 9: Infrastructure

Chapter 4

Disadvantages of Redevelopment

- Any lacuna in preparation of the Redevelopment Deed would result in a significant loss to the members who are eligible for many perks in consideration of giving permission for the project.

- For a considerable period of time, members are required to give up possession of their flats which disrupts their age-old routine.

- If converted to Commercial Complexes, Residential Complexes are seldom preferred for housing purposes or dwellings.

- Additional new members would take a longer time to gel with the original members, resulting in disputes on various issues.

- Additional members will require extra water consumption, creating scarcity or shortage of available water supply.

- Additional vehicles will require additional parking space.

- New construction is loaded with all kinds of modern amenities, which will, in turn, increase the cost of maintenance to be paid to the Society.

- The Tax burden is high, and in case the Occupation Certificate (OC) is not procured, Municipal charges and Water charges are also high.

- There is an increase in Property Taxes.

- The additional area received will attract Stamp Duty and Registration Charge at the current Market Price.

- There is always a fear of half way stalled project resulting in a Court case.

Chapter 5

Need for Redevelopment

As the words 'Redevelopment' suggests, it means developing something again.

As discussed in the previous chapter regarding Mumbai, the city and the metropolitan area have been developed exhaustively over the last few decades, due to which the availability of land has dwindled. This means that most of the kind of development the city sees is in the form of old buildings being replaced with new ones.

The main reasons for redevelopment include the following:

- Few developable open land parcels left:

  As already discussed, there are hardly any developable land parcels available in the city. Most of them have already been developed in the past decades

- Failure of schemes:

  SRA scheme, which was launched with much fanfare to solve the problem of slums in Mumbai, has been unable to solve the very problem. To date, there are many slums which are present across the metropolitan region, which houses a good chunk of the population of Mumbai, Dharavi being the prime example

Figure 10: Slums in Mumbai

- Few landlords own a huge chunk of land:

  A handful of individuals and trust own a huge chunk of Mumbai's habitable area. A preliminary survey carried out by SRA found that around 6,600 acres which represents approximately 20% of Mumbai's habitable area, were owned by just 9 Individuals and Trusts, most of which were Parsi's or trusts named and run after Parsi's, which shows the tryst of the community with Mumbai over the last century (TOI, 2015)

- Old and dilapidated buildings:

  Many buildings, especially the ones built in South Mumbai, were built over a century ago, during the British Raj. Most of them are not in good condition, structurally weak and dilapidated. They pose a huge threat to not only the people residing in the building but also to the people in the vicinity and the city at large

Figure 11: Old and Dilapidated Building

- Modern Housing needs:

  The décor, interiors, and architecture have all changed with changing times. As such need for new buildings, with modern houses, are needed.

  Buildings and complexes having modern amenities, open spaces, among others have become the bare minimum requirement in housing complexes, Covid 19 pandemic has only exemplified such needs

- Land Parcels which cannot be developed:

  There are many land parcels which, although lie vacant, have many regulations and problems facing their development. Some of them are as follows:

- Salt Pan lands:

  Which, although have been opened up for development but have yet not been taken up for development. A total of 5,400 acres of land is under salt pan in Mumbai City

Figure 12: Salt Pan Land

- Mangroves:

  A good percentage of land is under mangroves and cannot be developed so as to maintain a ecological balance and not further harm the environment. Mangroves are also play a key role by preventing flooding

Figure 13: Mangroves in Mumbai

- Textile and other mills:

  Many of these mills which were dotted across south Mumbai, saw development in the 1990s and 2000s, few of which are now left have a lot of litigation or are not developable

Figure 14: Textile Mills in Mumbai

- Encroachments on Land:

  Mumbai and Slums are almost always synonymous. These are illegally built on private or public land, on footpaths too.

Figure 15: Slums in Mumbai

The need for redevelopment is of acute importance, especially in a city like Mumbai, where there is no choice but to develop vertically, and that can only be attained after demolishing old structures and building new ones with modern amenities and facilities.

Chapter 6

Types of Development

While this is a broad-based distinction, we will be concentrating on two types of such development. Namely, Builder led development and Self-development.

As discussed in Chapter 1, in the early advent of development in Mumbai, the city saw self-development in the decades of 1960s till 1980s led by individuals and groups of individuals forming cooperative housing societies. Then came the Era of Builder led development which mainly gained pace in the 1980s and is the way development is done till now

Builder Led Development:

In this type of development, the building is developed by the builder, who takes care of everything from start to finish.

- Builder buys the land from a private party or the government authority.

- The builder may also go in for redevelopment by signing a Memorandum of Understanding (MOU) with the landlord/ owner of the building for the redevelopment.

- The builder may also go in for a JV with the landowner. This way of development has gained pace in the city in the last few years as builders shy away from blocking a huge chunk of capital in the form of land, instead choosing an asset-light approach and investing that money for building operations. Mumbai has seen good traction in this space, with many deals happening.

- After taking care of the land, the builder takes tenant permissions and applies for various permissions with the authorities such as BMC, among others.

- All the other functions and roles in the process are also carried out by the Developer, namely designing, operations, marketing, sales etc.

- Eventual sales and completion of the project are one of the last steps, but by far the most important one is getting the Occupation Certificate from the authorities, which signifies not only the completion of the project but also that the building has been constructed by adhering to the norms and laws laid down.

Self-Development:

In Self Development, it is usually the individual or a group of individuals who come together to construct a building

In this type of development, all the roles and functions typically done by the builder are now done by the individuals or the members themselves, i.e. all the functions right from the start to the end are now done by the members themselves, usually outside consultants and contractors are appointed to help them oversee, but the primary responsibilities fall on the members themselves

The dependency on the builder reduces, and the process becomes more transparent.

One of the main issues plaguing the sector today is unscrupulous builders who have often taken the customers, house owners, and old tenants for a ride by hiding crucial information, cheating, and defrauding them.

Another main issue is that of the delay in projects, it is seen that many times due to a mistake of the builder, lack of liquidity, and wrongful construction, among other reasons the project/ development comes to a standstill, this leaves the old tenants and new homeowners who have booked houses hanging in a lurch, in a helpless condition and many times at the mercy of the builder.

By choosing Self-development, the above two problems stated are mitigated and have other immense benefits too, which we will discuss in detail in chapters ahead.

Chapter 7

Steps in Builder Led Redevelopment

The list given below is usually the steps involved when a builder undertakes redevelopment; they are as follows:

- Buying rights to an existing Building by paying the landlord, getting into a JV or signing an MOU for redevelopment

- Getting the required tenant signatures to undertake redevelopment

- Appointing various stakeholders like consultants, architects, liaison etc.

- Approaching the authorities with regards to IOD/CC

- Commencing the project

- Undertaking marketing and sale of the flats/houses in the project

- Completion of the project and procuring Occupation Certificate

- Reconveying back the land to Society and procuring Building Completion Certificate

Chapter 8

Taxation Aspects

While undertaking a developing project various taxes are applicable, all these taxation aspects need to be studied closely as they ultimately have a bearing on the cost of the project and the financial for the stakeholders involved.

Goods and Services Tax (GST)

Tax Structure upto 31st March 2019

Sale of under-construction residential flats/units – 12% or 8% (with ITC)

Sale of under-construction commercial units – 12% (with ITC)

Works contracts - 18% (with ITC)

Joint Development – owner's share - 12% or 8% (with ITC)

Sale of completed flats/units - NIL (with ITC reversal)

Tax Structure from 1st April, 2019 onwards:

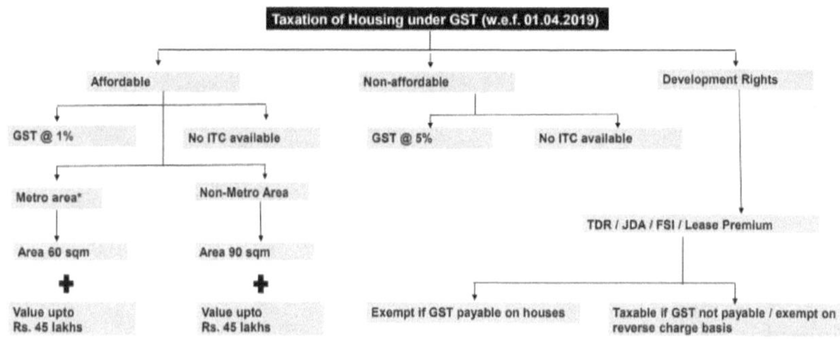

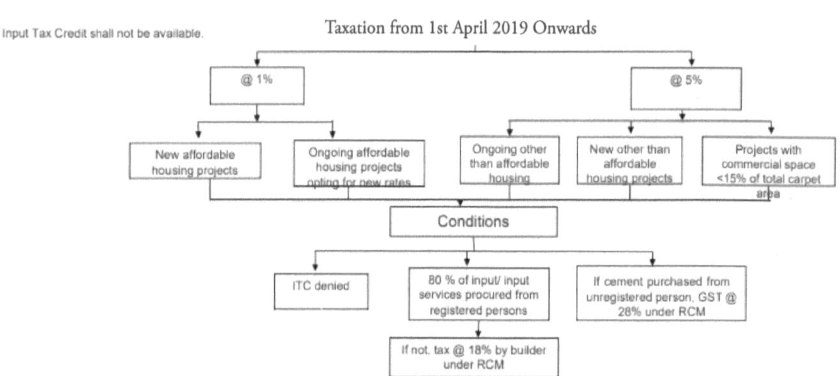

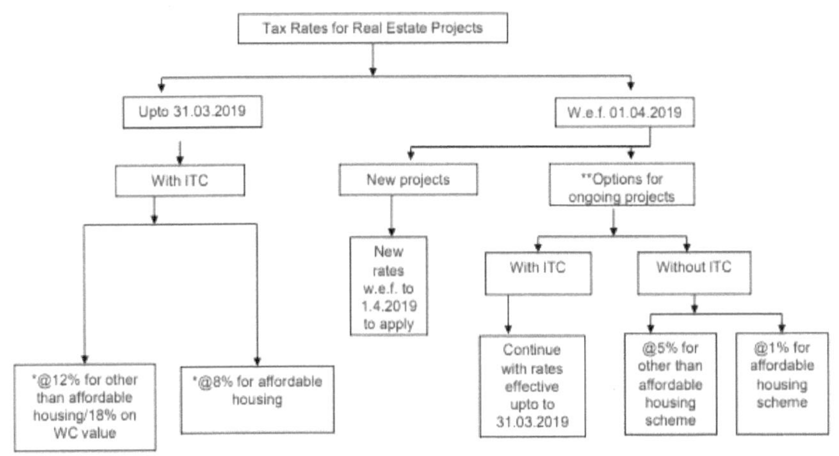

For any project of redevelopment of a Society, the following transactions, as per the Goods and Services Tax Act, 2017, are treated distinctly:

1. Supply of Transfer of Development Rights/Floor Space Index (commonly known as TDR/ FSI) by the society to a Developer

2. Supply of Residential units by the Developer to the society in lieu of supply of TDR/ FSI by the Society

3. Sale of Residential units by the Developer to outsiders

4. Sale of Commercial units by the Developer to outsiders.

Redevelopment of a Residential Society by a Developer (Classified as an RREP):

- Supply of Transfer of Development Rights/Floor Space Index (commonly known as TDR/ FSI) by the society to a Developer.

  Before 01/04/2019, Supply of Transfer of Development Rights/FSI was levied @ 18 % and payable by society under forward charge, and the liability would arise at the time of receipt of completion certificate or first occupancy whichever is earlier.

However, after 01/04/2019, vide Notification No. 03/2019 CT(R) dated 29th march 2019 applicability of GST in a Residential Real Estate Project (RREP) on supply of transfer of development rights/ FSI by the society to a developer is as elicited below. A "Residential Real Estate Project (RREP)" shall mean a REP in which the carpet area of the commercial apartments is not more than 15% of the total carpet area of all the apartments in the REP, where in REP means "Real Estate Project (REP)" as defined in section 2 of the Real Estate (Regulation and Development) Act, 2016.

When the /society provides Development Rights (TDE/ FSI) to a Developer, such a transaction is exempt from payment of GST on the condition that the flats constructed by utilization of such TDR/FSI are booked before receipt of completion certificate or first occupancy, whichever is earlier.

Thus, if there are any flats which remain un-booked on the date of receipt of completion certification or first occupancy, GST shall be payable at the rate of 18% on the value of TDR proportionate to the carpet area of un-booked flats subject to maximum 1 % / 5% of the value of such un-booked flats.

The liability to pay GST shall arise at the time of receipt of completion certificate or first occupancy, whichever is earlier and payable by the Developer under Reverse Charge Mechanism (RCM).

The total taxable value of TDR/ FSI will be equal to the rate of the flats sold to dependent buyers nearest to the date of the development agreement.

- Supply of Residential units by the Developer to the society in lieu of supply of TDR/ FSI by the society.

In a development project, the Developer gets the development rights from the society and in turn, he gives flats to them. This is a barter of supplies; here, there is no consideration in the form of money.

However, for the purposes of levy of GST, the value of services has to be quantified. Therefore, the law provides that in such cases, the value of construction service, i.e. flats supplied to society, shall be equal to the rate of the flats sold to independent buyers nearest to the date of the development agreement.

GST shall be payable by the Developer at the effective rate of 1%/5% at the time of receipt of completion certification or first occupancy, whichever is earlier.

- Sale of Residential units by the Developer to outsiders

  For Flats sold by the Developer, to other customers, before receipt of the Completion Certificate, GST will be chargeable at the effective rate of 1%/5% (after taking into consideration 1/3rd abatement in value towards cost of land) by the Developer. For flats sold post receipt of Completion Certificate, the same shall be exempt from payment of GST. The liability to charge and pay GST, a rise sat the time of receipt of every instalment/payment* (refer to Section 31(5)).

- Sale of Commercial units by the Developer to outsiders

  As any REP having commercial up to 15 % of the total carpet area of all the apartments in the REP is defined as RREP. Therefore, the commercial units in the RREP GST is chargeable at the concessional rate of 5% and payable at the time of receipt of every installment/payment*(refer to Section 31(5))

Stamp Duty:

Whenever a property transaction takes place or changes hand, a charge known as stamp duty is payable to the Municipal Authority. This is payable in case of all types of property transactions, like for new properties or old and existing ones being exchanged between two or more parties. Further duty is payable across all asset classes.

In Mumbai a stamp duty of a total of 6% is now payable, which until 31st of March 2022 was at 5%. The additional 1% is towards the metro cess introduced by the Maharashtra government in the cities of Mumbai, Pune and Nagpur

Figure 16: *Stamp Paper*

Section B

Redevelopment Checklist

Chapter 1

Is Redevelopment Necessary

Societies must carefully evaluate whether redevelopment is truly necessary, by keeping few points in mind, some of them are listed below:

- Societies should assess the actual condition of their buildings. If structural audits indicate that the building is beyond repair and in a dilapidated state, only then should redevelopment be considered

- Clear title of the land belongs in the name of society

- Conveyance of the said land and building have been done in name of the society and its registered with appropriate authorities

- No internal litigation exists and there is consent preferably from all or atleast majority flat owners for redevelopment

- Before approaching developers, societies should do a feasibility check themselves by appointing a PMC, to help them understand how much extra area and other specifications as regard to new development can be achieved

- Societies to prioritize the developer's track record and ability to deliver, rather than simply choosing the one offering the most space

- Societies which hire a PMC for this regard, can put various filters such as technical and financial capabilities

- Society members should have following basic requirements:
  - Extra Space over and above current flats
  - Rentals during the construction period, payable in advance or not
  - Corpus amount for old tenants, payable in advance or not
  - Floor to Floor Height for each flat
  - Floors on which old tenements will get their houses on
  - No of Car Parks and type of parking
  - Amenities provided
  - Timeline of construction and completion
- Society should also focus on quality living and density of flats after redevelopment as usually the number of flats not only increase but the people living in same society and sharing the space and amenities also increases
- Lesser aspects which should also be given importance include:
  - sewage and drainage systems,
  - better energy efficiency
  - incorporate sustainable technologies, such as solar panels and rainwater harvesting

Chapter 2

Checklist of applicable Acts and Rules

1. Arbitration Act

2. Company Act

3. DCPR: Development Control & Promotion Regulation Rules (DCPR 2034)

4. Fire Act: Maharashtra Prevention of Fire & Life safety Measures Act

5. GST

6. Income Tax

7. Indian Contract Act

8. Indian Registration Act

9. Maharashtra Stamp Act

10. Maharashtra Revenue Code

11. MRTP: (Maharashtra Regional Town Planning Act)

12. MMC ACT: (Mumbai Municipal Act)

13. MCS Act & Rule

14. Partnership Act

15. RERA

16. SRA / MHADA as & where require

17. Society's Registered Byelaws

18. The Maharashtra (Urban Areas) Preservation of Tree Act

19. The State of Maharashtra Unified Development Control & Promotion Regulation (UDCPR 2020)

20. The Workmen's Compensation Act

21. Transfer of Property Act

22. Tree Act: The Maharashtra (Urban Areas) Preservation of Tree Act

23. ULC: Urban (Land & Ceiling & Regulation) Act

Chapter 3

Basic Points to make a Feasibility Report

Feasibility Report is a report which gives an understanding of how much development potential a plot has and other information necessary for the society to make a decision as to the redevelopment of the project

- Latest and updated Property card

- Conveyance Deed or Lease Agreement

- Survey Number, Plot Number, Milkat Number, Gat Number

- List of members with their respective Unit's details

- Occupancy Certificate

- Sanctioned Plan Copy

- Latest D.P. Remark

- Latest Survey Report for Society's Land / Plot

- Ward in which society falls

- Road width of the road abutting the site

- Zoning of the land

- Class I or Class II land

- Relevant DCPR Provision with respect to FSI and development potential

Chapter 4

Query Checklist

- Additional Area Provided (MOFA or RERA): Specify the extent of extra area granted under the Maharashtra Ownership Flats Act (MOFA) or the Real Estate Regulatory Authority (RERA).

- Additional Benefits for Old Buildings: Discuss any extra benefits for redeveloping older buildings that are likely to be demolished.

- Additional Car Parking Purchase: Confirm if members can purchase extra car parking spaces and understand the process.

- Acquiring Land from MHADA/BMC: Clarify the types of land that can be acquired from MHADA and BMC for redevelopment purposes.

- Amenities for the Society: Learn about the additional amenities provided to the entire society.

- Amenities List: Ensure that the amenities offered by the builder are detailed and comprehensive.

- Architect Considerations: Ensure the architect reviews key factors before the builder provides a final quote.

- Architect Review: Ensure the architect reviews all key factors before the builder provides a final quote.

- Agreement Copy: Request a copy of the agreement proposed between the developer and new flat purchasers.

- Agreement Structure: Determine whether there will be a common agreement for all societies or separate agreements.

- Bonafide vs. Provisional Members: Seek clarification on the rights of Bonafide Members versus Provisional Members regarding their ability to attend and vote in Special General Body Meetings.

- Car Parking Allocation: Discuss the number of car parking spaces allocated to each member.

- Car Parking Space Sizes: Review the sizes of car parking spaces reserved by the developer for existing members.

- Communication After Demolition: Develop a communication plan to be implemented following the demolition.

- Compliance with Section 79A of the MCS Act: Confirm with the Managing Committee if they are adhering to Section 79A of the MCS Act.

- Construction Bar Chart: Request a detailed bar chart outlining the various stages of construction.

- Construction Schedule: Obtain a detailed schedule for the construction process, including key milestones and deadlines.

- Corpus Fund: Clarify the corpus fund amount that the developer will provide to the society.

- Cost for Higher Floor Flats: Reconfirm the additional cost for flats on higher floors.

- Developer Charges: Clarify the charges paid by developers to individual members and their payment frequency.

- Dish Antenna on Terrace: Inquire if a dish antenna will be installed on the terrace.

- Extra Amenities for Buyers: Identify any additional amenities provided to individual flat purchasers.

- GST During Redevelopment: Understand the GST implications related to the redevelopment process.

- GST on Resale: Determine if GST will be applicable when reselling the flats.

- GST Responsibility: Identify who will be responsible for paying the Goods and Services Tax (GST) for the new flats.

- Handling Requests for Additional Area: Find out how requests for extra area will be managed and accommodated.

- Income Tax Implications for Members: Discuss the income tax implications, such as Long-Term Capital Gains (LTCG) Tax, for individual members if the redevelopment project is delayed beyond three years from the date of the Permanent Alternative Accommodation Agreement.

- Income Tax Implications for the Society: Clarify if the society will incur income tax liabilities, such as LTCG, due to project delays beyond three years from the date of the Development Agreement.

- Key Features of Redevelopment: Learn about the main features and benefits of the redevelopment project.

- Land from MHADA/BMC: Clarify the types of land available from MHADA and BMC for redevelopment purposes.

- Loan Estimates: Estimate the loan amounts flat purchasers can expect to receive.

- NOC for Bank Loans: Discuss how to manage flats with existing bank loans and who will obtain the No Objection Certificate (NOC) from the bank.

- Number and Location of Buildings: Understand how many buildings will be constructed, their proposed locations, and view any visual representations.

- Number of Floors: Confirm the total number of floors in the new buildings.

- Occupants' Rights: Request clarification from the Managing Committee and Developer on the rights of all occupants, including provisional members, nominees, legal heirs, and family members, ensuring equal benefits.

- Parking Allocation and Sizes: Discuss and confirm the number and sizes of car parking spaces allocated to members.

- Plot Amalgamation Process: Discuss the procedure for amalgamating plots for redevelopment, if applicable.

- Pocket Terraces: Confirm whether individual flats will include pocket terraces.

- Procedure for Vacating Flats: Seek clarification from both the Managing Committee and the Developer on the procedure for vacating flats, including the timing and process involved.

- Progress Chart: Request a bar chart outlining the redevelopment progress, including timelines for documentation, Initial Occupancy Document (IOD), and commencement certificate.

- Procedure for Vacating Flats: Seek clarification from the Managing Committee and Developer on the procedure for vacating flats, including timing and process.

- Precautions During Redevelopment: Discuss the precautions that the society should take during the redevelopment process.

- Registrar Approval: Verify if registrar approval is required for the redevelopment process.

- Sample Agreements: Request samples of various documents such as the Conditional Consent Letter (I) & (II), Development Agreement, Indemnity Bond, Bank Guarantee, Permanent Alternative Accommodation Agreement, and Agreement for Sale.

- Set-Off Against Rent and Corpus: Find out if there is an option to offset rent and corpus amounts for those purchasing additional area to reduce tax liability.

- Society Office: Check if there will be a dedicated office space for the society within the new development.

- Stamp Duty for Additional Area: Clarify how stamp duty will be assessed for any additional area purchased by individual members.

- Stamp Duty on Development Agreement: Understand the stamp duty implications for the development agreement signed by the society.

- Stamp Duty Responsibility: Clarify who will bear the cost of stamp duty for the new flats.

- Stamp Duty Rights for Women: Clarify the rights and entitlements of women regarding stamp duty payments.

- Tax Implications for Corpus and Rent: Discuss the tax implications and taxability of the corpus fund and rent received.

- Tax Planning Advice: Seek guidance on effective tax planning strategies for the society during the redevelopment process.

- Termination Clause: Ensure a termination clause is included in case the builder fails to meet their commitments.

- Termination Due to Delays: Clarify the society's right to terminate the agreement if the builder causes significant delays.

- Title Clearance Certificate: Discuss the importance of obtaining a title clearance certificate before commencing the redevelopment.

- Three-Phase Electric Meter: Confirm whether each flat will be equipped with a three-phase electric meter.

- Transfer to Legal Heirs: Ensure there is a clear process for transferring flats to legal heirs or nominees if a member dies during redevelopment.

- Transportation Charges: Understand the transportation charges covered by the developers and their payment schedule.

- Video Updates: Arrange for regular video updates on construction progress to be shared via the WhatsApp group.

- WhatsApp Group: Set up a WhatsApp group for direct communication between members and the builder.

Chapter 5

Analysis of 79 A Process

Section 79 A of the Maharashtra Co-operative Societies Act, 1960 deals with the redevelopment process of a society building

It gives clarity and transparency as to the redevelopment process of the society and also the smooth functioning of a society.

Earlier, there were hardly any standard practices, no prescribed guidelines, little to no transparency, confusion and litigation when it came to the redevelopment of a society.

With regards to this, the Government of Maharashtra issued a circular dated 3rd January 2009 under section 79 A of Maharashtra Co-operative Societies Act, 1960 to bring clarity and transparency to the whole process of redevelopment of society.

Major complaints when it comes to redevelopment are as under:

- Lack of transparency in the redevelopment process

- Appointment of Contractors in a haphazard manner

- The members are not taken into confidence in the process of redevelopment

- Violations of the provisions in the Co-operative Act, Rules and Bye-Laws

- Lack of coordination between various internal stakeholders like Architects and Project Management Consultants

- Project Report is not prepared

- Proper Procedure for finalizing tenders is not followed

- Nexus between the managing committee members and Developer

- There is no uniformity in agreements with Developers

In order to deal with the above problems, the Government came out with the circular; the circular laid down the following:-

1. To call a special general body meeting of the society to discuss the redevelopment of the society's building/s.

    No less than ¼ members of the society, the building of which is to be redeveloped, should submit a requisition to the Secretary or the Managing Committee elected as per provisions of Bye-Laws and lawfully formed along with their suggestions for the redevelopment of the society's building for convening Special General Body Meeting to finalize the policy on the redevelopment of the building.

2. To call the special general meeting

    On receipt of the application, as stated in clause one above, Managing Committee should take a note thereof within eight days, and the Secretary of the society should convene a Special General Body Meeting of all the members of the society, Agenda of the proposed Meeting should be furnished to each member 14 days prior to the day of meeting and acknowledgement thereof should be kept on record of the society.

3. To receive written suggestions for the members on the redevelopment of the building

    Before convening the said meeting, society should obtain a list of Architects / Project Management Consultants on the panel of Government / Local Authority and obtain quotations from a minimum of five experienced and expert persons for preparing a project report for redevelopment work of the building and one expert person from among them will be selected in the Special General Body Meeting. The following business will be transacted in the said Special General Body Meeting:

- To take preliminary decision by considering the members' demand for redevelopment of society's building and suggestions received in respect of the same.

- To select expert and experienced Architect / Project Management Consultant on the panel of the Government / Local Authority for work of redevelopment of the building and to finalize items of work to be done by them and terms and conditions of work.

- To submit an outline of the programme for redevelopment of the building.

- To accept written suggestions from members relating to the redevelopment of the building. Members of the Society will be entitled to submit in writing to the committee eight days prior to the meeting their realistic scheme, Suggestions and recommendations for redevelopment of the building in the name of an experienced and expert Architect / Project Management Consultant known to them. However, that Architect / Project Management Consultant should submit a letter that he is desirous of doing work of redevelopment.

4. Decisions to be taken in the special general meeting

The quorum for the Special General Body Meeting convened for the redevelopment of the building of the Co-operative Housing Society will be ¾ of the total members of the society. If a quorum is not formed, the meeting will be adjourned for eight days, and if there is no quorum for the adjourned meeting, it will be deemed that members are not interested in the redevelopment of the building, and meeting will be cancelled.

On the formation of the quorum for the meeting, Suggestions, recommendations and objections from all the members with regard to the redevelopment of the society's building will be taken into consideration and opinions expressed by all the members will be recorded in the minute's book with names of concerned members. Therefore a preliminary decision will be taken on whether to redevelop society's building or not. Such a decision must be taken with a majority vote of more than ¾ of the members. On preliminary resolution about doing the work of redevelopment getting passed, the following business will be transacted in the meeting.

- To select an expert and experienced Architect / Project Management Consultant from the Government / Local Authority panel for work of redevelopment of the building and to finalize items of work to be done by him and terms and conditions for the same.

- To submit an outline of the programme for redevelopment of the building.

5. To circulate the minutes of the meeting to all the members.

    Secretary of the Society should prepare minutes of Special General Body Meeting as above within ten days, and a copy thereof should be furnished to all members and acknowledgement, therefore, be kept on record of the society. Also, one copy should be forwarded to the office of the Registrar.

6. To issue a letter of appointment to the Architect / PMC

    The Secretary of the society will, within 15 days of the meeting, issue an Appointment Letter to the Architect / Project Management Consultant selected in Special General Body Meeting, and the society will enter into an agreement with Architect / Project Management

Consultant incorporating therein terms and conditions approved in Special General Body Meeting.

7. The initial work to be carried out by the Architect / PMC

    Work to be done in the initial stage by Architect / Project management consultant:

    - To survey society's buildings and land.

    - To obtain information about the conveyance of land to the society.

    - To take into consideration the prevailing policy of the Government and the regulations applicable from time to time depending on ownership of the land (MHADA/SRA/ Municipal Corporation) and to obtain information about FSI and TDR, which would be available in relation to building and land of the society.

    - To take into consideration suggestions and recommendations from the members for redevelopment of the building as also the residential area to be made available to the members, commercial area, vacant area, garden, parking, building specifications etc. and to prepare a realistic project report.

    - The architect / Project Management Consultant should prepare the project report within two months of the date of his appointment and submit the same to the committee of the society.

8. Business after receipt of the redevelopment project report

    Action to be taken on receipt of redevelopment Project Report:

    - On receipt of the Redevelopment Project Report as above, the Secretary of the society will convene a joint meeting to approve the Project Report with a majority vote by taking into consideration suggestions received from Committee Members and Architect / Project Management Consultant.

Notice in that behalf will be published on the Notice Board of the Society, mentioning the time, venue etc., of the meeting. It should be mentioned in the notice that a copy of the Project Report is available in the society's office for members to see, and the notice should be served to all the members that they should submit their suggestions eight days prior to the next Committee Meeting and acknowledgement of such notice should be kept on record of the society. Even days prior to the joint meeting, suggestions received from the members will be forwarded by Society's Secretary to the Architect / Project Management Consultant for his Information.

- There will be a detailed discussion in the Joint meeting on the suggestions/recommendations from members and the opinion thereon of the Architect / Project Management Consultant, and the project report will be approved with necessary changes. Thereafter draft of the tender form will be prepared, and the date of the next joint meeting will be fixed for discussion on the draft tender form and finalizing the same. While preparing the draft tender form, in order to get competitive quotations from renowned experts and experienced developers, either carpet area or corpus fund fixed (not to be changed) and by finalizing other technical matters, the Architect / Project Management Consultant will invite tenders. Society's members will be entitled to furnish information about it to the reputed and experienced developers known to them.

9. To Publish a list of Tenders Received

- On the last day for receiving quotations, the Secretary of the Society will prepare a list of offers received and display the same on the notice board of the society.

- After 15 days of the last day for receiving quotations, the Secretary of the society will convene a special meeting of the Managing

Committee of the society. Authorized representatives of bidders and members of the society desirous of remaining present can remain present for the meeting as observers. Tenders so received will be opened in the presence of all, and the Architect / Project management consultant will scrutinize all tenders and prepare a comparative chart after checking merit, reputation, experience and comparative rate etc. and select a minimum of five bids and if the bids received are less than 5, all the bids for putting up before Special General Meeting and concerned bidders will be informed about it immediately.

10. Selection of a Developer

- The office of Registrar to appoint an Authorized Officer for the SGM.

   An application with a list of the members should be sent within eight days to the registrar for the appointment of an authorized officer to attend the Special General Meeting of the Society for selecting a Developer out of those selected by the committee of the society with the help of the consultant, by taking into consideration his experience, merit, financial capacity, technical capacity and competitive rate etc.

- To call SGM to finalize the tender.

   After the appointment of an authorized officer, with his prior permission Secretary of the Society will fix the time and venue to convene Special General Body Meeting for the appointment of the Developer and the Agenda of this meeting will be sent to all the members 14 days prior to the meeting by hand delivery and by registered post and keep acknowledgement thereof on record of the society. Also, the office of the Registrar will make arrangements to keep his authorized representative present for the meeting. Also, arrangements will be made for video shooting of the meeting at the cost of the society. Any person other than formal members will not be entitled to attend this meeting.

Therefore, members will be required to present at the venue of the meeting with their Identity Cards. At the time of submitting the redevelopment proposal to the concerned authority for sanctioning, selection of Developer and other work should have been done in the presence of an authorized officer from the Registrar's office.

- If there is no quorum for SGM.

  If the quorum of ¾ members out of the total members is not formed for Special General Body Meeting, the meeting will be adjourned for eight days. Suppose a quorum does not get formed for the adjourned meeting. In that case, it will be deemed that the members have no interest in the redevelopment of the building, and the meeting will be cancelled, Thereafter the said subject will not be taken up before the Special General Body Meeting for approval.

- The business in the SGM for selection of the Developer.

  In the Special General Body Meeting to be convened for the selection of Developer, an authorized representative from the office of the Registrar will be present and observe the proceedings of the meeting. Also, on concerned representatives and authorized officers remaining present at the venue and at the time of the meeting and on a quorum of ¾ members getting formed, the following business will be transacted in the meeting.

  Providing comparative information in respect of tenders selected for presentation (for redevelopment work).

  Presentation by bidders one by one. To select a Developer for redevelopment of the building, to finalize terms and conditions and finalize the tender.

  To obtain consent from the selected Developer.

Give information about further work. It will be essential to take written approval by ¾ majority vote of the members present for the meeting for selection of Developer. If the selected Developer or his representative does not remain present for the meeting, further action will be taken by presuming that they have given their consent for the project.

11. Development agreement to be executed

Subject to the terms and conditions approved by the General Body Meeting of the Society, an agreement should be entered into with the Developer within one month under guidance from the Architect / Project Management Consultant. Along with the points suggested by the Architect / Project Management Consultant appointed by the society, the following points will also be included in the agreement.

The period for completing the redevelopment project of the society will not exceed more than two years, and in exceptional cases, it will not exceed three years.

The developer will give a Bank Guarantee for an amount equal to 20% of the project cost. During the period of redevelopment, the Developer will make available to the members' alternative accommodation in the same area as far as possible or arrange to pay monthly rent and deposit as acceptable to members or make available transit camp accommodation.

The said agreement will be registered under Registration Act, 1908. Upon completion of the redevelopment project, new members will be admitted to the society only with the approval of the General Body Meeting of the Society.

The carpet area to be allotted should be clearly mentioned in the agreement. Development rights vested in the Developer will be non-transferable. Members will vacate their respective premises only after all legal approvals are received for the redevelopment of the building.

The rights of those who are in possession of the flats will remain unaffected. If any dispute arises in the work of redevelopment, provision should be made in the agreement to resolve the same as per provisions of Section 91 of the Act.

After receipt of the Occupation Certificate, flats in the redeveloped building should as far as possible be allotted as per present conditions floor-wise, and if it becomes necessary to allot flats by drawing lots, on completion of construction, the Developer should make arrangements drawing lots, and at that time flats should be allotted in the presence of Registrar's representative and this process be recorded by video shooting.

12. Any Committee member or Office Bearer of the Society should not be the Developer or relative of the Developer.

13. Building plans sanctioned by the Municipal Corporation / Competent Authority should be put up before the General Body Meeting for information, and if any member wants copies of approved documents, he should submit an application for the same to the society, and it will be binding on the committee to furnish the information by charging a necessary fee. By order and in the name of the Governor of Maharashtra

The above directives were issued in the public interest and, more particularly, in the interest of both members and committee members of Co-operative Housing societies for better implementation of the redevelopment proposal. **It is to be noted that the 79A process is not mandatory for Redevelopment.** Furthermore, with 51% consent, redevelopment can proceed without any legal hassles or hurdles.

Chapter 6

Consent and Dissenting Members

In redevelopment there is majority consent needed to go ahead with development. In all societies, there will be people who are dissenting and not open to idea of redevelopment.

Sometimes the members are dissenting due to arbitrary and illegal decisions by Managing Committee of their society. In such cases members should present their case properly:

- Should be well aware of the acts and regulations in place including 79A process

- Should cross verify if any violations have taken place against any of the applicable acts or regulations

- Should prepare their case well and should take other members into confidence

- Timely complaint should be raised within the society and escalated further if needed

- Complaint can also be filed with relevant authorities with timely follow-ups in place

- Subject matter experts should be consulted to prepare a fool proof case

Chapter 7

Document Checklist

Documents required to start a Redevelopment process:

1. Society Registration Certificate.
2. 7/12 Extract.
3. Form no. 6 from Revenue Office.
4. Conveyance Deed / Lease Deed / Sale Deed.
5. Search Report and Title Certificate.
6. Index II
7. N. A. Order.
8. Development Agreement.
9. City Survey Plan.
10. Approved Building Plan.
11. Copy of IOD.
12. Commencement Certificate.
13. Occupation Certificate.
14. Completion Certificate.
15. Agreement for Sale.
16. Stamp Duty paid proof.

17. Registration Charges paid proof.

18. Appointment Letter.

Documents needed to be prepared for Redevelopment:

1. Feasibility report.

2. Suggestions from members.

3. Public Notice for inviting the Tender.

4. Minutes of various meetings.

5. Correspondence with different Authorities.

6. Obtaining required permission from Deputy Registrar, BMC, ULC Department, NA Department etc.

7. Tender Form.

8. Summary of Tenders received.

9. Approval of Tenders in the General Body meetings and preparation of Draft and Final Minutes.

10. Appointment letters to Advocate, Structural Engineers, Architect, Project Management Consultant etc.

The Developer has to arrange the following documents:

1. Partnership Deed of the Developer duly registered OR Memorandum of Association (as the case may be)

2. Copy of Registration Certificate.

3. Name and address of the Partners / Directors along with their PAN.

4. Copy of PAN of the Firm.

5. Income Tax Return filed for the last three years of the Partners / Directors of the Company.

6. Service Tax Registration no.

7. Copy of Balance Sheet and P/L A/c to understand the financial strength of the Firm / Company.

8. Feasibility Report from the Developer as to how they would develop the Property at the offers given by them

Agreements to be prepared:

1. Redevelopment Agreement.

2. Indemnity Bond by the Developer.

3. Format of Bank Guarantee from the Developer.

4. Power of Authority from the Society to the Developer.

5. Agreement for alternate accommodation.

6. Consent Letters from the members of the Society.

7. Consent Letters from the members of the Society to Builder / Developer / BMC.

8. Memorandum of Understanding (MOU) between the Society and Builder / Developer.

9. Appointment Letter from the Society to the Builder / Developer.

10. Possession Letter from the builder to the Members.

11. Application by new members to the Society for becoming members in Form No. 3.

12. Undertaking from the new members of the Society.

13. Format of the Resolution to admit new members.

14. List of Documents required to be collected from the builder.

15. Revocation / Cancellation of Power of Attorney.

(Source: ICAI)

Chapter 8

Stakeholder Checklist

Following is a brief list of the stakeholders involved in a Redevelopment Project:

- Landlord/owner
- Old tenants
- PMC
- Architect
- Lawyer
- Chartered Accountant
- RCC Consultant
- Landscaping Consultants
- Government / Statutory Authorities
- Customer/ Home Owners
- Brokers / Channel Partners
- Financial Institutions
- Vendors

Dangerous and Dilapidated Projects

Chapter 1

Dangerous and Dilapidated Structures

Every year the Municipal cooperation and other authorities publish a list of buildings which they categorize as C1.

In this category, the buildings which so fall, are declared as Dangerous to stay in and should be vacated. These are Dilapidated Structures which don't need urgent repair but need to be broken down and redeveloped and are unsafe to stay in their present condition.

List of C1 Category Structures in Mumbai City as of April 2024:

List of C1 Category Dangerous and Dilapidated Buildings in Mumbai as on

23-Apr-2024

Sr No.	Ward	Beat No.	Name of Building	Address
1	A	226	Meher Mansion	Cooperage Road, Colaba, Mumbai 400 001
2	A	225	Noble Chamber	Janmabhomi Marg, Fort, Mumbai 400 001
3	A	225	J.K. Somani	British Hotel lane, Fort, Mumbai-400 001
4	B	224	Parekh Chamber	125-127 Sheriff Devji Road, Mumbai-400003
5	B	224	296 Samuel Street Mumbai-400009	296 Samuel Street Mumbai-400009
6	C	222	Sheel Bhavan	Building no 14, 4th marine Street, Dhobhi talav, Mumbai _02
7	D	217	M/s. Shalimar Exhibitors	335, Shalimar House, M.S. Ali Road, Grant Road (E), Mumbai.
8	D	217	Lohana Mahaparishad Bhuvan Building	10, 4th Khetwadi Lane, S.V.P. Road, Mumbai- 400 004.
9	D	214	C.S. No. 3A/730 of Tardeo Division, 136, Sarvodaya Estate, Sarvodaya Mills Compound, Mumbai-400 034.	Besides Urmi Aangan Building, Mumbai-400 034.
10	D	219	Two nos. of structures (Garages) of Mayfair Complex, Little Gibbs Road, Malabar Hill, Mumbai-400 006	Little Gibbs Road, Malabar Hill, Mumbai-400 006
11	D	219	51-C, Amritsarwala Punjabi Walkeshwar Dharmashal Sanitarium Trust Building, Backside of Banganga Dispensary, Banganga, Mumbai-400 006	Walkeshwar Dharamshala Sanitarium Trust Building, Backside of Banganga Dispensary, Banganga, Mumbai-400 006.
12	D	219	Bhatiya Niwas, Banganga Cross lane , mumbai -400006	Banganga Cross lane , mumbai -400006
13	D	218	Mehta Mahal	Mathew Road, Charni Road, Mumbai-400004
14	D	217	Novelty Cinema	M.S. Ali Road, Mumbai-400007.
15	D	215	Transit Camp No. 9 & 10	Tulsiwadi, Tardeo, Mumbai-400034.
16	E	207	TRIVENI APARTMENT	NEAR MAKBA CHAWL, S BRIDGE, BYCULLA (W), MUMBAI-400011
17	E	211	BOMBAY SOAP FACTORY	HUSAINI BAUG, MADANPURA, MUMBAI-400008
18	FS	200	Ambedkar Bhavan,	Gokuldas Pasta Lane, Dadar (E)
19	FS	204	Laisha Baba Dargah Road	Tawripada, Dr. S. S. Rao road, lalbaug, Mumbai 400012
20	GN	192	Khandke Bldg. No. 07 & 08	R.K. Vaidya Marg, Dadar (W), Mumbai-400 028
21	GN	190	Girikunj Building SAC No. GN1602770020000	L.J. Road, Mahim, Mumbai-400 016
22	GN	190	30, Rail View Building SAC No. GN1607620160000 B - GN1607620080000	Senapati Bapat Road, Opp. Mahim Station, Mahim, Mumbai-400 016
23	GN	190	White House	F.P. no. 534/A4, TPS III, C.S. no 1205, Sonawala Agiyari Lane, Mahim (W), Mumbai 16
24	GN	191	Janardan Apartment A,B,C,D,E, & G Wings	F.P. No.886, Shankar Ghanekar Marg, Dadar (W), Mumbai-28
25	GN	192	Shri Samarth Vyayam Mandir	P.L. Kale Guruji Marg, Dada (West), Mumbai-400028
26	GN	190	Calcutta Confectionery &Shitladevi Industrial Estate	, 140, Sitladevi Temple Road, Maim, Mumbai- 400 016. (Gr. + 1)
27	GS	195	Madhusudan Mill 1st & 2nd Building from North West Side situated along with Shankarrao Naram Path	C. S. No. 445, Shankarrao Naram Path, Lower Parel, Mumbai - 400 013

List of C1 Category Dangerous and Dilapidated Buildings in Mumbai as on

23-Apr-2024

28	HE	87	Kalika Niwas	Nehru Road, Santacruz East, Mumbai- 400 055
29	HE	90	Rathod Mansion	Rathod Mansion Kalina Kurla Road, Kalina, Santacruz (East), Mumbai 400 029
30	HE	91	Yousef Building	Yousef Building, PJ Nehru Road, Santacruz (East), Mumbai – 400 055.
31	HE	91	Airview A wing Zaitun Villa Building	Air View A wing and Zaithoon Villa .T.S.No. 2459 to 2468,2469A & 2527B, of village Kolekalyan, Nehru Road, Opp.BMC Market, Santacruz (East) , Mumbai- 400 0.
32	HE	94	Krishna Kunj	Krishnkunj Apartment Golibar, Oppsite to Kabristan, Santacruz (East.), Mumbai
33	HE	87	D'Souza Mansion	Plot No. 58, TPS-V, Prabhat Colony, Santacruz (E) Mumbai 400055.
34	HE	88	Shanti Sadan	Ashok Nagar, Vakola, Santacruz (E)
35	HE	90	Kailas Parbhat	Kailas Parbhat CHS, CST road, Kalina, Santacruz (E)
36	HE	87	Rakesh Kunj	F.P. No.50, TPS-V, Prabhat Colony, Santacruz E
37	HE	91	Sabha building	Near Nityanand hotel, CST road, Kalina, Santacruz East
38	HW	97	K. B. Lal Industries	Linking road extension, Santacruz West, Mumbai- 400054.
39	HW	98	Vora building	2nd Hasnabad lane, Khar(W),Mumbai 400 054
40	HW	98	Riviera CHSL	15th road, Off North Avenue road, Santacruz(W), Mumbai-54
41	HW	98	Leela Niwas	plot no 83/C5, Meera Baug, 17th road, Santacruz(W), Mumbai-54
42	HW	100	Fantasia building	C/1224, Village Bandra, Sherley Rajan rd, bandra W
43	HW	101	Serenity building	CTS no. 1037B, 9th road, near almeida park, bandra west, Mumbai- 400050
44	HW	101	Plot no.42, Chimbai	plot no. 42, Chimbai, Bandra West, Mumbai- 400050
45	HW	101	Akbar Villa,	Plot No.83, 83A, CTS No.B26, Hill Road, Bandra West Mumbai-50
46	HW	98	Jitendra Building	Plot No.276, Near Madhu Park, 12th road, Khar (W), Mumbai-52
47	HW	100	Lily villa, off Sherley rajan rd	Sherley Rajan Road, Bandra (W), Mumbai 400050
48	HW	102	Bangdiwal chawl	64,66,68,bangdiwala Chawl,Plot bearing A/525 & A/528 bazar raod,bandra west,mumbai-50
49	HW	101	Plot No.77/A	Waroda Road, Bandra West, Mumbai - 400050
50	HW	98	Sunkist	Plot no 47, St. Joseph road, Santacruz west, Mumbai-400054
51	HW	100	Mangal Saran	16th Road, Khar West, Mumbai-52.
52	HW	101	Dalhoff Bunglow	The St. Sebstian Homes CHSL, Plot no. 11, CTS No. B-513, St. Roque Road, Bandra(W), Mumbai-50.
53	KE	81	Bunglow No.124,Shaheed Bhagat Singh CHSL	Plot No.104,AG Link Road Andheri east mumbai
54	KE	72	Ganga Niwas	Near Jogeshwari Railway Station, Caves Road, Jogeshwari East, Mumbai- 400 060
55	KE	85	Vhanavati Bunglow	F.P. No. 469, Azad Road, Vileparle (E), Mumbai-400057.
56	KE	85	Evergreen CHSL	402, TPSV, N.P. Thakkar Road, Vile Parle (E), Mumbai - 57
57	KE	85	Mani Bhuvan	M.G. Road, Vile Parle (E)
58	KE	79	Agarwal Bhavan	Plot No. 48, Sher-E-Panjab, Andheri (East), Mumbai- 400 069
59	KE	85	Jaal Hotel	Junction of Nehru Road and Western Express, Vileparle (East), Mumbai- 400 057
60	KE	79	Anand Vihar	Plot No. 39/40, Sher-E-Punjab Society, Opposite Sher-E-Punjab, Gurud wara, Andheri (E), Mumbai- 400093
61	KE	75	Mehru Manzil	Church road, marol, Andheri east
62	KE	72	Smrutee Building	Hindu Friends Society Road, Near Saraswati Bag Municipal School, Jogeshwari (East), Mumbai- 400 060
63	KE	85	Laxmi Sadan	Laxmi Sadan, FP 330, Nariman Road Off Nehru Road, Next to Chaksi Bhuvan, Vileparle (East), Mumbai- 400 057

List of C1 Category Dangerous and Dilapidated Buildings in Mumbai as on				
23-Apr-2024				
64	KE	85	Mahavir Darshan	Mahavir Darshan CHS.Ltd. Off. P.M. Road, Vileparle (East), Mumbai- 400 057
65	KE	85	Clyde Bunglow	Misquitta Street, Azad Road, Vileparle (East),Mumbai-400057
66	KE	81	Cicila Sagar CHS,	CTS No. 444, Village Kondivita, Near, Wireless Station, Junction of Shriniwas Bagarka Road, and Wireless Road, J.B. Nagar, Andheri (East), Mumbai.
67	KE	83	Dreamland CHS. Ltd.	Cardinal Gracious Road, CTS No. 600, Village-Chakala, Andheri (East), Mumbai 400 099
68	KW	60	Vijay Bharat CHS LTD, Near Sai Iconic Building, Four Bunglow, J. P. Road, Lokhandwala Complex, Andheri (West), Mumbai-400 053	Vijay Bharat CHS LTD, Near Sai Iconic Building, Four Bunglow, J. P. Road, Lokhandwala Complex, Andheri (West), Mumbai-400 053
69	KW	65	Andheri Purab Paschim CHS, 217, Gilbert Hill Road, Behind Andheri Recreation Club, Andheri (West), Mumbai-400 058	Andheri Purab Paschim CHS, 217, Gilbert Hill Road, Behind Andheri Recreation Club, Andheri (West), Mumbai-400 058
70	KW	65	Bunglow no. 1 (Pathare Prabhu Trust), Plot no. 25, CTS no. 148, TPS-II, J.P. Road, Near Navrang Cinema, Andheri (West), Mumbai-400 058	Bunglow no. 1 (Pathare Prabhu Trust), Plot no. 25, CTS no. 148, TPS-II, J.P. Road, Near Navrang Cinema, Andheri (West), Mumbai-400 058
71	KW	66	Munshi Bhavan, JP Road, Andheri (W), Mumbai	Munshi Bhavan, JP Road, Andheri (W), Mumbai
72	KW	67	Bindra Niwas, Opp. Sport Complex, J. P. Road, Andheri (W), Mumbai	Bindra Niwas, Opp. Sport Complex, J. P. Road, Andheri (W), Mumbai
73	KW	67	Keval Kunj, Plot no.18, Gulmohar Cross Road no. 12, JVPD Scheme, Vile Parle (West), Mumbai-400 049"	Keval Kunj, Plot no.18, Gulmohar Cross Road no. 12, JVPD Scheme, Vile Parle (West), Mumbai-400 049"
74	KW	67	Namita Building., plot no. 9, CTS no. 9A/3/3/1, Gulmohor Cross Road no.4, JVPD Vile Parle West, Mumbai-400 049	Namita Building., plot no. 9, CTS no. 9A/3/3/1, Gulmohor Cross Road no.4, JVPD Vile Parle West, Mumbai-400 049
75	KW	67	Kashivishwanath Building Residential CHS LTD, plot no. 46 of village Juhu, Tal. Vile Parle, N. S. Road no.7, JVPD Scheme, Vile Parle West, Mumbai-4000 49	Kashivishwanath Building Residential CHS LTD, plot no. 46 of village Juhu, Tal. Vile Parle, N. S. Road no.7, JVPD Scheme, Vile Parle West, Mumbai-4000 49
76	KW	67	Hem Niketan, situated on plot no. 5, Suvarna Nagar Society, JVPD, Vile Parle West, Mumbai-400 049	Hem Niketan, situated on plot no. 5, Suvarna Nagar Society, JVPD, Vile Parle West, Mumbai-400 049
77	KW	68	Gunvant Villa 'Ulka Palace' Plot no. 8, CTS no. 1278, Survey no. 82 of village Versova, Seven Bunglow, Mumbai-400 061	Gunvant Villa 'Ulka Palace' Plot no. 8, CTS no. 1278, Survey no. 82 of village Versova, Seven Bunglow, Mumbai-400 061
78	KW	68	Nazneen Bungalow, Seven Bungalows, Versova, Andheri (West), Mumbai-400 058	Nazneen Bungalow(Shanti Niwas), Seven Bungalows, Versova, Andheri (West), Mumbai-400 058

List of C1 Category Dangerous and Dilapidated Buildings in Mumbai as on

23-Apr-2024

79	KW	68	Ratan Kunj Bunglow situated at 7 bunglow, Versova, Andheri (West), Mumbai-400 061	Ratan Kunj Bunglow situated at 7 bunglow, Versova, Andheri (West), Mumbai-400 061
80	KW	69	Chandan Cinema, CTS No.38-A, Village Juhu, Juhu, Mumbai-400049	Chandan Cinema, CTS No.38-A, Village Juhu, Juhu, Mumbai-400049
81	KW	70	Vainatheya CHS ltd, 192-B, S.V. Road. Irla, Vileparle (West) Mumbai 58.	Vainatheya CHS ltd, 192-B, S.V. Road. Irla, Vileparle (West) Mumbai 58.
82	KW	70	Shanti Villa, Jn. of Dadabhai Road & Bajaj Road, Vile Parle (West), Mumbai - 400 056	Shanti Villa, Jn. of Dadabhai Road & Bajaj Road, Vile Parle (West), Mumbai - 400 056
83	KW	71	Vraj Kunj CHS LTD, 28, Vallabhbhai Patel Road, Vile Parle (West), Mumbai-400 056.	Vraj Kunj CHS LTD, 28, Vallabhbhai Patel Road, Vile Parle (West), Mumbai-400 056.
84	L	162	Kanthariya Stable	Jarimari, Andheri Kurla Road
85	L	162	Kuldeep Silk Milk	MTNL Road,Sakinaka
86	L	162	Johnson and Johnson	Near Bacchu Garage, Sakinaka, Mumbai
87	L	166	Janki Niwas,	Bailbazar, Kurla (W)
88	L	167	Jairaj Bhuvan Building,	New Mill Road, Kurla(W0
89	L	168	Sakharwala Building.	Kurla court
90	ME	144	Anusaya Niwas	Anusaya Niwas Building, Survey no.34, Near Lijjat Papad Co. Borla, Govandi (E), Mumbai-400088
91	MW	152	Plot No-35	Sindhi Imegrants CHS, Chembur, Mumbai-71.
92	MW	152	Yadukul Bldg	Postal Colony Road, Plot No. 24, Chembur
93	MW	152	Kamal Sadan	Plot no. 8, Sindhi Society, Ekveera Marg, S.T. Road, Chembur, Mumbai-71
94	MW	152	Plot No 278	Saint Anthony Road, Chembur, Mumbai
95	MW	152	Singhavi Apartment (Supreme House)	Road no.16
96	MW	152	Kashi Niketan	N G acharya marg
97	MW	152	Krishna Baug bldg no. 1 and 4	R.C. Marg
98	MW	152	Shree Sai Sadan	12th Road, Chembur, Mumbai
99	N	130	Shanta Bhuvan	situated at Gangawadi, L.B.S. Road, Ghatkopar (W), Mumbai – 400 086
100	N	129	Narayan Nagar Building No. 1	Narayan Nagar, L.B.S. Marg, Ghatkopar (W), Mumbai – 400 086.
101	N	132	Janjira Chawl	Rajawadi Rd.No.1, Ghatkopar(E).
102	N	130	Gopal Bhuvan	L.B.S.Road, Ghatkopar(W).
103	N	130	Tin Bunglows	CTS No. 3320 to 3336 of Ghatkopar Kirol Village, J.V. Road, Khot Lane, Ghatkopar (W), Mumbai - 400 086.
104	N	128	Giridhar Nagar Building	Giridhar Nagar Building Jivdaya Lane Ghatkopar (W)
105	N	130	Milan shopping center	Narayandas Morardasji Building (Milan Shopping Centre), M.G Road, Ghatkopar (W), Mumbai-400086
106	N	128	patidar building	near telephone exchange jivdaya Lane ghatkopar west
107	N	128	Hira bhavan	LBS ROAD, near jiniva hospital, ghatkopar West
108	N	130	Nathalal bhuvan	Gangawadi, LBS ROAD, Ghatkoapar West
109	N	132	Jamnadas umarshi trust building	M.G.ROAD, GHATKOPAR EAST OPP AMBIKA DARSHAN BUILDING
110	N	132	The ghatkopar parimal building chs ltd	Vikrant circle, R B Mehta marg, Ghatkopar east

List of C1 Category Dangerous and Dilapidated Buildings in Mumbai as on

23-Apr-2024

111	N	132	Parekh marke premises chs Ltd A wing (G+3), B wing (G+2), C wing (G+2),D wing (G+1)	M.G.ROAD, GHATKOPAR EAST
112	PN	46	Dev Niwas	Mamletdar Wadi, Cross Road no.3. Malad (W), Mumbai – 400 064
113	PN	46	Ismail Baug	Opp.Malad Railway Station, Anand Road, Malad (W). Mumbai – 400 064
114	PN	46	Desai House	P.G.Road, Somwari Bazar, Malad (W), Mumbai – 400 064
115	PN	47	Diamond Apartment	Padma Nagar, New Link Road Malad (W), Mumbai– 64
116	PN	46	Vinayak Sadan	Liberty Garden Road no.1, Malad (W). Mumbai – 400 064
117	PN	46	Sai Zaruka	B.J.Patel Road, Malad (W), Mumbai – 400 064
118	PN	46	Somaiya Shopping Center	Sainath Cross road, Malad (W), Mumbai – 64
119	PN	46	Harjivandas	Ramchandra Lane, Malad(W), Mumbai- 400 064
120	PN	46	Smita Building	Ramchandra Lane, Malad(W), Mumbai- 400 064
121	PN	46	Sai Mangal CHSL	Opp.Malad Railway Station, Malad (W), Mumbai – 400 064
122	PN	46	Shree Rani Sati Nagar CHSL (Bunglow)	G plot, Rani Sati Nagar, S.V.Road, Malad (W)
123	PN	46	Indian Oil Corporation Ltd	S.V.Road, Malad (W), Mumbai – 400 064
124	PN	46	Nandanvan CHSL	Ramchandra Lane, Malad (W), Mumbai – 400 064
125	PN	49	Porocol House of Our Lady Of Sea Church	Madh Island, Madh road, Malad West
126	PN	32	Annie J. Barretto House no. 83	CTS No.169 of Village Malwani, Kharodi, Off.Marve Road, Malwani, Malad (W), Mumbai – 400 095
127	PN	36	Pushpa Park, G Plot (G+2)	Near S.K. Patil Hospital, Daftary Road, Malad(E), Mumbai- 400 097
128	PN	44	Mistry bhuvan	r.s. marg. opp. Raheja tipko, Malad East
129	PN	45	Bhupendra Niwas	Jitendra Road, Malad(E), Mumbai- 400 097
130	PN	36	Hawa Hira Mahal	Daftary Road, Malad (E), Mumbai - 400 097
131	PN	36	'Sahkar Bhuvan'	bearing CTS No. 249, 249/1 to 13 situated at Khandwala Lane, Malad (E), Mumbai – 400 097
132	PN	45	Shri Jain Dharmik Shikshan Society	Jitendra Road, Malad (E), Mumbai – 400 097
133	PN	43	Tapovan Deep CHSL	Western Exp.Highway, Off.Rani Sati Marg, Behind RBI Quarters, Pathan Wadi, Shivaji Nagar, Malad (E), Mumbai – 97
134	PS	55	Gajanan Building No.9, .	CTS no. 34 village Pahadi Eksar, Jawahar Nagar, Goregaon(W)
135	PS	55	Manibhuvan Builidng	S. V. Road, Goregaon (W), Mumbai 400 104.
136	PS	55	Aashish Building	S. V. Road, Opp. Vijay Sales, Goregaon (W), Mumbai 400 104.
137	PS	55	Prabhu Niwas, Plot No. 99,	Jawahar Nagar, Road No. 10, Goregaon (W), Mumbai-400104
138	PS	55	Laxmi Niwas Building	Tilak Nagar, Near Bhosle Marg, Goregaon (W), Mumbai-400104
139	PS	51	Kundan	J. P. Road No. 03, Goregan (E), Mumbai
140	PS	51	Samadhan	J. P. Road No. 03, Goregan (E), Mumbai
141	PS	54	Ameer Mansion	92, Jay Praksha Nagar, Goregaon (East), Mumbai – 400 063
142	RC	15	Multani Chawl Structure No. 390	F.P. No. 58, TPS-III, S.V.Road, Umed Ashram, Borivali (W.), Mumbai - 92.
143	RC	15	Multani Chawl Structure No. 391	F.P. No. 58, TPS-III, S.V.Road, Umed Ashram, Borivali (W.), Mumbai - 92.
144	RC	15	Multani Chawl Structure No. 392	F.P. No. 58, TPS-III, S.V.Road, Umed Ashram, Borivali (W.), Mumbai - 92.
145	RC	15	Multani Chawl Structure No. 393	F.P. No. 58, TPS-III, S.V.Road, Umed Ashram, Borivali (W.), Mumbai - 92.
146	RC	15	Ram Nagar Trust 1, Bldg. 1	Ram Nagar Road, S.V. Road Borivali west, mumbai 92.
147	RC	15	Ram Nagar Trust 1, Bldg.2	Ram Nagar Road, S.V. Road Borivali west, mumbai 92.

List of C1 Category Dangerous and Dilapidated Buildings in Mumbai as on

23-Apr-2024

148	RC	15	Gyan Nagar CHS Ltd.,	Shree Vardhman Sthankwadi Jain Sangh, L.T. Road, Opp. Diamond Talkies, Borivali (West), Mumbai - 400 092
149	RC	13	Satyabhama niwas Building no. 02	Kasturba road no. 01, behind kasturba police station, Borivali East. Mumbai-400066.
150	RC	13	Satyabhama niwas Building no. 01	Kasturba road no. 01, behind kasturba police station, Borivali East. Mumbai-400066.
151	RC	15	Ganesh Bhuvan	F.P. No. 7, Opp. Thakkar Mall , S.V. Road, Borivali West. Mumbai-400 092
152	RC	15	Laxmi Bhuvan	F.P. No. 6, Opp. Thakkar Mall , S.V. Road, Borivali West, Mumbai-400 092
153	RC	17	Gitesh Haresh Dawankar Chawl Vishnu Niwas	TPS-III, F.P. No. 664, R. M. Bhattad Road, Borivali (West), Mumbai - 400 092
154	RC	13	Trimurti C.H.S. Ltd.	Carter Road No 3, Borivali (East), Mumbai - 400 066
155	RC	15	Gulab Mansion	Maharashtra Nagar, Maharashtra Nagar Lane, Borivali West
156	RC	15	Siddharth Borivali CHS	Factory lane, LT Road, Borivali West. Mumbai - 400 092
157	RC	16	Indrapuri CHS	Indrapuri Building, Jayraj Nagar, Opp. MHB Police Station, Link Road, Borivali West, Mumbai - 400091.
158	RC	13	Geeta Bhavan	Carter road no. 6, Borivali East
159	RC	13	Amba Bhavan	Carter Road No 7, Borivali (East), Mumbai - 400 066
160	RC	10	Himmat Nagar CHS	CTS No. 447/2 of Village & Taluka Borivali, Gymkhana Road, Near MCF Club, Borivali West, Mumbai - 400092
161	RN	8	Shiv Guru CHSL	Jaywant Sawant Road, Dahisar West
162	RS	30	"Paradise Building",	Shantilal Modi Road, Kandivali (W), Mumbai -400067.
163	RS	30	Kunti Deep	Iraniwadi Road no. 3, Kandivali (W), Mumbai- 400067
164	RS	30	Vijay Mahal	Kasturba Road, Kandivali West
165	RS	22	Sai Hevan	Poisar, S.V.Road, Kandivali (W)
166	RS	30	Sukan CHS ltd	CTS No 1180, MG Cross Road No 3), Kandivali(W
167	RS	30	Kanti terrace	Station Road, S.V. Road, Kandivali (W), Mumbai-67
168	RS	24	Jai Hind Dal mill	Fonseca Compound, Akurli Road, Kandivali (E), Mumbai-101
169	RS	30	Kalpataru CHSL.	Mathuradas Road, Opp. Panjab National Bank, Kandivali (W), Mumbai-67
170	S	112	Kamal Vihar	kamal vihar LBS marg bhandup West 78
171	S	117	Sujal apartment no.4 CHSL	plot no 87, Datar colony, Bhandup (E), Mumbai
172	S	111	Ulwekar Building	behind Ravi Swagat CHSL, Bapusaheb Juvekar Marg. Bhandup(E),Mumbai-42
173	T	105	Shyam Bhuvan	Shyam Bhuvan Gokhale Road, Mulund (E). Mumbai-81
174	T	105	Sotta Bhuvan and Jalaram Bhuvan	L. T. Road, Off Railway Station, Mulund (E)
175	T	105	Abhijeet building	Abhijeet building , BK road mulund (E)
176	T	106	Laxmi Chhaya	Laxmi Chhaya Bldg, Navghar Galli No. 1, Navghar Road, Mulund (E),
177	T	107	Ramani Bhuvan	Ramani Bhuvan, R.R.T. Road, Mulund (W).
178	T	107	Bramhajyoti	Bramhajyoti Bldg. B (Mirani Nagar), Ganesh Gawde road, Mulund (w).
179	T	107	Mahamaya	Mahamaya Bldg, Ganesh Gawde road, Mulund (w).
180	T	107	Vallabh Bhuvan	Vallabh Bhuvan,Cross Walji Laddha road, Mulund (W),
181	T	107	Ekvira Sadan	Ekvira Sadan 'Mulund (W),N.S. Road, Mulund (W). Mumbai-400080
182	T	107	Pushpa Niwas	'Pushpa Niwas' (A &B) wing, M.G.Road, and R.P.Road Junction, Mulund(W), Mumbai-80
183	T	107	Giriraj Brijwasi Bhavan	Giriraj Brijwasi Bhavan, 'B' Building, CTS No.1342B, Dr. Gajanan Purndare Marg, Off Valji Laddha Road, Mulund (W), Mumbai-400080

List of C1 Category Dangerous and Dilapidated Buildings in Mumbai as on

23-Apr-2024

184	T	104	Mahadev Niwas	Mahadev Niwas', Junction of R.H.B.Road & S. L. Road, Mulund (W), Mumbai - 400080.
185	T	107	Bal Smruti Biilding	Bal Smruti Building', Murar Road, Mulund (W), Mumbai - 400080.
186	T	103	'Sushila Sadan'	'Sushila Sadan' Gaiwala Building, M.G.Roadl, Mulund (W), Mumbai-400080.
187	T	103	Pragji Sunderji (Mochi) Building	Pragji Sunderji (Mochi) Building Plot No.821, N.S.B. Road, Near Mulund Police Station, Mulund (W), Mumbai-400080
188	T	107	Neelketan Building	Neelketan Building CTS No.1454A, Kasturba Road, Mulund (W), Mumbai-400080

MHADA 79 A

The President of India on December 02, 2022, assented to the bill proposing amendments to the Maharashtra Housing and Area Development Act, 1976 ("**the Act**"), and introduced the Maharashtra Housing and Area Development (Amendment) Act, 2020 ("**Amendment Act**"), thereby clearing the way for the redevelopment of `cessed' and `dangerous' buildings.

Cessed buildings are those that are maintained and repaired by the Mumbai Building Repair and Reconstruction Board (MBRRB) of MHADA, for which tenants pay cess to the housing authority. They are developed under 33(7) regulation of the DCPR 2034. There are 3 categories of cess buildings – CAT A, CAT B and CAT C depending on the age of the buildings. Cess Buildings are more than 50 years old and are in urgent requirement of reconstruction since repairs is not a permanent solution. Cess buildings are found in Island City of Mumbai that is from Mahim to Churchgate and Sion to Colaba.

Section 79A mandates compulsory redevelopment for cessed buildings declared dangerous by MHADA or its repair board. Property owners receiving such notices have three months to initiate redevelopment, after which occupants have an additional six months to propose redevelopment if the owner fails to act.

Background:

The presidential approval of the Amendment Act comes in the backdrop of a two-year waiting period since the bill was first approved in the Maharashtra State Assembly on September 08, 2020.

According to the Government of Maharashtra, a large number of buildings in Mumbai are categorized as cessed buildings. Despite declaring these cessed buildings as dangerous by the Mumbai Municipal Corporation under Section 354 of the Mumbai Municipal Corporation Act1 ("**MMC Act**"), the landowners have failed to undertake the redevelopment of such cessed and dangerous buildings on a priority basis.

By way of the Amendment Act, Section 79A has been introduced which deals with the redevelopment of cessed buildings that are declared as dangerous by the Mumbai Municipal Corporation under Section 354 of the MMC Act ("**Building/s**"). The Amendment Act allows the owners of the Buildings to initiate the process of redevelopment within 3 months from the date of receipt of notice under Section 354 of the MMC Act. In the event, the redevelopment process is not initiated within 3 months, the Maharashtra Housing and Development Authority ("**MHADA**") will issue another notice to the owners of the Buildings allowing them to submit a redevelopment proposal within 6 months from the date of receipt of the notice. The redevelopment proposal shall be accompanied by the consent of 51% of the occupants or tenants in the Buildings.

In the event the owners fail to do so, the proposed co-operative housing society of tenants or occupants will be entitled to submit a redevelopment proposal within the next 6 months with the consent of 51% of the occupants or tenants in the Building. In the event, the tenants or occupants also fail to make a proposal, MHADA will undertake redevelopment of incomplete or stalled projects as per the procedure laid down in Section 91-A of the Act.2 Further, the Amendment Act provides that once the building is redeveloped by the proposed cooperative housing society or MHADA, the owner will get compensation at the rate of 25% of the amount of the ready reckoner rates or 15% of the built-up area of sale component determined as per the ready reckoner rates, whichever is higher.

The Bare Act:

"**79-A.** (*1*) Notwithstanding anything contained in sub-section (*3*) of section 88 and section 92 of this Act and sections 354 and 499 of the Mumbai Municipal Corporation Act, in case of the building to which the

provisions of sub-section (*1*) of section 82 applies (hereinafter in this Act referred to as "cessed building"), which is declared dangerous by the Mumbai Municipal Corporation under section 354 of the Mumbai Municipal Corporation Act or by the competent authority, if the redevelopment of such building is not taken up by the owner or landlord of the cessed building, within three months from the date of issue of notice under section 354 of the Mumbai Municipal Corporation Act by the Mumbai Municipal Corporation or the competent authority, the Board may adopt the following procedure:–

(*a*) a notice shall be issued to the owner or landlord of the cessed building to submit the proposal for redevelopment within six months from the date of issue of notice. Alongwith the proposal, consent of fifty-one per cent. of the occupants or tenants of the said building shall be accompanied;

(*b*) if the owner or landlord fails to submit the proposal within the period and the manner as provided in clause (*a*), the proposed co-operative housing society of the occupants or tenants of such building may submit the proposal to the Board, for redevelopment of such building under the relevant provisions of the Development Control and Promotion Regulations-2034 for Greater Mumbai, within six months from the date of communication received from the Board. The proposal shall be accompanied with the consent of at least fifty-one per cent of the occupants or tenants:

Provided that, when the building is redeveloped by the proposed co-operative housing society, the compensation to the owner or landlord shall be paid by the concerned co-operative housing society as per the provisions of sub-section (*2*);

(*c*) if the redevelopment is not initiated within the period and manner as provided in clauses (*a*) and (*b*), the Board shall reconstruct the building by acquiring such building, without insisting on consent of at least fifty-one per cent of the occupants or tenants of the said building.

(*2*) When the building is redeveloped under the provisions of clauses (*b*) and (*c*) of sub-section (*1*), the compensation shall be paid to the owner or landlord, at the rate of twenty-five per cent. of the amount of Ready Reckoner Rates, determined under the Maharashtra Stamp (Determination of True Market Value of Property) Rules, 1995 of the open land of such building or fifteen per cent. of the built-up area of sale component determined as per the Ready Reckoner Rates, whichever is higher.

Explanation.– For the purposes of this sub-section, "sale component" means the built-up area remaining after deducting Rehab Built-up Area from the permissible Built-up Area admissible as per the relevant provisions of the Development Control and Promotion Regulations-2034 for Greater Mumbai.

(*3*) If the building is redeveloped by the Board under clause (*c*) of sub-section (*1*), subject to the provisions of sub-section (*2*) for payment of compensation, the provisions of sections 92 and 93 shall *mutatis mutandis* apply, for acquisition of such building.".

"**91-A.** Notwithstanding anything contained in any of the provisions of Chapter VIII or any other law for the time being in force or in any agreement, contracts, judgment, decree or order of any Court or Tribunal to the contrary, in cases where, after obtaining No Objection Certificate for redevelopment of old cessed building as per the Development Control and Promotion Regulations-2034 for Greater Mumbai or any other earlier Development Control Regulations therefor, the building is demolished and,–

(*a*) the redevelopment work is left incomplete, delayed or has not been commenced within three years from the date of issue of No Objection Certificate; or

(*b*) the redevelopment work of old cessed building is stalled for more than two years from the date of issue of the Commencement Certificate by the Mumbai Municipal Corporation or Planning Authority; or

(*c*) the holder of the No Objection Certificate has committed breach of any of the terms and conditions of the No Objection Certificate or has not paid rent for temporary alternate accommodation to the tenants or occupants of such building,–

the Board may, after obtaining the prior approval of the State Government, initiate the action for acquisition of such building under the provisions of the Act and shall complete the redevelopment work.".

In section 95-A of the principal Act,–

(*1*) in sub-section (*1*),–

(*a*) for the words and figures "not less than 70 per cent." the words and figures "not less than 51 per cent." shall be substituted;

(*b*) in the proviso, after the words "temporary accommodation" the words "or to pay rent in lieu thereof" shall be added;

(*2*) in sub-section (*3*), after the words "summary eviction" the words "or be shifted in Board Transit Camp wherever available" shall be added.

Legal Update:

Bombay High Court has directed MHADA to form guidelines to declare a building dangerous / dilapidated after it came to its notice that several properties have been hastily declared as dangerous/ dilapidated relying solely on visual inspection. Accordingly SOPs to 79A were framed as:

A. a) Deputy engineer / executive engineer should inspect the building and inspection report as well as according to the monsoon survey report ensure whether building is hazardous (video graphing and photographing should be done.)

B. b) Then architect should do the inspection and prepare the repairing estimate and if residents do not submit the additional amount on PCL within the prescribed time period or if the structural repair cost is not affordable, then to avoid loss of life and finances warning notice should be given that the building is hazardous and instructions should be given to vacate the building. If residents, tenants, and apartment owners of the buildings have objected to this notice and submitted the essential amount for the structural repair work within the prescribed time period, then the required repairs should be done. However, if this amount is not submitted, a structural inspection of the building is to be done, and according to the report, if the building is in a hazardous condition, the following action is to be taken.

1. 1. Ensure whether Greater Mumbai Municipal Corporation has issued notice to expel the dangerous part of the building under the section 354 of the Greater Mumbai Municipal Corporation?

2. 2. After confirmation about the dilapidated and hazardous condition of the building, a notice according to the 79 A (1) should be given to the owner about the building has been dangerous or hazardous to the health and safety of the residents.

3. 3. If owner do not comply to the notice given by Greater Mumbai Municipal Corporation according to the section 354 of the Greater

Mumbai Municipal Corporation Act, 1988 or by the Mumbai Building and Reconstruction Board under 79 A (1) within three months, then concerned executive engineer should issue redevelopment notice to the owner according to the 79 A (1a).

4. 4. If owner do not submit the redevelopment project within 6 months or building owner haven't received expected consent letter from residents, then concerned deputy chief engineer should take combine hearing of the owner and residents according to the reference 1 and 2 and try to facilitate the redevelopment of the hazardous cess received building, the deputy chief engineer should approve orders according to the quality of the case.

5. 5. If the owner of the hazardous cess received building do not submit the redevelopment project within 6 months, then to do the redevelopment by the planned cooperative housing society of the residents or tenants concerned executive engineer should issue the notice according to 79 a (1B) to them. At the end of the six-month period, orders should be issued after hearing from the concerned tenants or residents.

6. 6. IF the owner or planned cooperative housing society of the residents or tenants do not submit the redevelopment project within 6 months then Mumbai Building and Reconstruction Board should acquire the land under 79 A (1) and take action for redevelopment of this building.

G. c) In the cases where the landowner has already been given notice according to Section 79 a (1a), action should be taken according to the first point (b) and then directly at points 4, 5 and 6.

In the case of received redevelopment projects, action should be taken according to dates 16.08.2010, 05.11.2020, and 05.03.2021, as per quality.

The Supreme Court Test:

The Maharashtra government came up with a law for acquiring old and dilapidated buildings that were unsafe as the tenants were sitting tight over the properties and landlords had no money for repairs, the Supreme Court observed while examining whether privately owned resources can be considered "material resources of the community".

Chief Justice D Y Chandrachud made the observations while dealing with a host of petitions filed by landlords who are up against the Maharashtra law. He is heading a nine-judge constitution bench which is considering the vexed question arising from the petitions about whether private properties can be considered "material resources of the community" under Article 39 (b) of the Constitution, which a is part of the Directive Principles of State Policy (DPSP). Article 39(b) makes it obligatory for the State to create policy towards securing "that the ownership and control of the material resources of the community are so distributed as best to subserve the common good".

Invoking the obligation under Article 39(b), the MHADA Act was amended in 1986. Section 1A was inserted into the Act to execute plans for acquiring lands and buildings in order to transfer them to those needy and in possession of such lands or buildings. The amended law has Chapter VIII-A with provisions allowing the state government to acquire cessed buildings and the land they are built on if 70 per cent of the occupants make such a request.

The Property Owners Association has challenged Chapter VIII-A claiming that the provisions discriminate against the owners and violate their right to equality under Article 14. As many as 16 petitions including the lead petition filed by the Mumbai-based Property Owners Association (POW) was heard by the bench which also comprised Justices Hrishikesh Roy, BV Nagarathna, Sudhanshu Dhulia, JB Pardiwala, Manoj Misra, Rajesh Bindal, Satish Chandra Sharma and Augustine George Masih.

The lead plea was filed by POW way back in 1992 and it was referred thrice to larger benches of five and seven judges before being referred to a nine-judge bench on February 20, 2002. The CJI referred to the distinction between a case of a private person as opposed to title in the community. He gave the example of private mines and said, "They may be private mines. But in a broader sense, these are material resources of the community. The title may rest in a private individual but for the purpose of Article 39 (b), our readings should not be constricted but must have that broad understanding." "Take a case like these buildings in Mumbai. Technically, you are right that these are privately owned buildings, but what was the reason for the law (MHADA Act)… we are not commenting on the legality or the validity of the law that will be tested independently," the CJI said.

"The reason why the state legislature came out with this (Act) was that these are old buildings of the 1940s…With a kind of monsoon in Mumbai, these buildings get dilapidated because of the saline weather," Justice Chandrachud said. He referred to the meagre rent being paid by tenants, especially in Mumbai, living in these old buildings. "Because, honestly, the fact that the rent was so meagre that the landlord said no, they had no money at all actually to repair them…and (with) the tenants sitting tight, no one would have the wherewithal to repair the whole building and hence the legislature came up (with the Act)," the CJI said. Elaborating on the phrase 'material resources of the community', the bench said the community has a vital interest, and if a building falls, the community is directly affected.

There are around 13,000 cessed buildings in Mumbai which need restoration or reconstruction. However, their redevelopment is often delayed due to differences between tenants or between owners and tenants on appointing a developer. At the outset, Solicitor General Tushar Mehta, appearing for the Maharashtra government, told the bench that "the only issue that has been referred to a larger Bench of 9-judges is whether the expression 'material resources of the community' under Article 39 (b) covers privately owned resources or not." The top law officer also said, "It is clear that the un-amended Article 31-C, to the extent upheld by the judgment in the Kesavananda Bharati case, is valid and in operation". The historically acclaimed 1973 Kesavananda Bharati judgement on "<u>basic structure</u>" doctrine had clipped the vast power of Parliament to amend the Constitution and simultaneously gave the judiciary the authority to review any amendment. At the same time, the 1973 verdict also upheld the constitutionality of a provision of Article 31-C, which implied that amendments for implementing the DPSP, if they do not affect the 'basic structure' of the Constitution, shall not be subjected to judicial review (Indian Express).

The Judgement is kept in "Reserve" and is expected before the retirement of CJI, 10th November 2024.

Section D

Reviving Stalled Projects

Meaning of Stalled Project

————— ❖❖ —————

Stalled projects are those projects which are incomplete despite crossing over their decided timelines, i.e. either obligations or promises made to allottee or time line defined during project registration even after exhaustion of extension u/s 6 or 7(3) of RERDA, 2016.

In Maharashtra, we have an acute problem with regard to the stalled project, and now data of lapsed projects are made available in the public domain for the caution of the allottee or prospective buyers. Nearly 10-15 % of total projects registered have been displayed as lapsed projects requiring the immediate attention of the Maharashtra Real Estate Regulatory Authority.

Reasons for projects getting stalled

Here we will understand the main reasons why the projects get stalled, there are many reasons for a project getting stalled and while they vary project to project, we have covered all the major ones, due to which the project gets stalled and stuck.

Unauthorised Construction:

As seen for many projects, developers undertake development without due permissions from all the departments; often, the developers don't want to wait and get stuck in the red tapism. As is widely known, it takes a lot of effort to get your file moved in various government departments, so many times, construction is carried on without due permission and approvals in place.

But when the authorities are intimated or get aware, a 'show cause notice' or 'stop order' notice is issued, halting the project and, as such, delaying it.

Many times the project is also in violation of various laws, most importantly the environment laws, construction is carried on without due approval, but once it gets stuck due to this reason, it takes a lot of time for the file to get cleared in the department and for the project to restart, many times the violations are so extreme in nature that the project gets stalled for a very long period of time.

Non-refundable fees:

For undertaking redevelopment of any kind, several permissions are needed for authorities for which various different fees are charged. Even for availing of extra FSI, premiums are needed to be paid.

Often these fees are non-refundable in nature, irrespective of whether the project is completed or not, as they are to be paid in advance.

Low velocity of Sales:

Due to the slowing down in the industry, consolidation and cut throat competition, many builders face the problem of sales.

Low velocity of sales or bookings can slow down and even stall the projects. This is because many developers rely on cash flows generated from the project itself to fund the construction activities.

Low velocity of sales can also be due to the project not being up to par, its location, surroundings, and builder name being tainted among others.

External Factors that adversely affected many projects:

1997-1999:

1. Overleveraging
2. Overtrading
3. Increase in TDR prices
4. Recession due to international reasons
5. Underworld threats

2004-2005:

1. HC Order in PIL over 154 unauthorised projects

2. Shortage of labour due to political reasons leading to a multifold increase in prices

3. Introduction of High-Rise permission but delay in implementation

2008-2012:

1. Change in policy – introduction of fungible FSI and delay in clearance of issues

2. Many changes related to SRA Schemes

3. The negative impact of the collapse of Lehman Brothers, sub prime mortgage

4. Scrappage of ULC Orders and mutation of entries in revenue records

5. Security issues due to terror attacks

6. Mosquitoes related epidemic

7. Water crisis due to drought

2013:

1. SC Judgment in Kohinoor case over two side open space for fire engine

2. Announcement of increase in FSI in Mhada projects but implemented after years

3. Policy paralysis

4. Change in civil aviation rules

5. Forest Land

2016:

1. Stay in PIL on the dumping ground

2. Changes in the environmental clearance committee

3. Changes in the use of TDR by linking it with road width and delay in clarity over the layout

4. HC Order in PIL over violation of civil aviation rules

5. Announcement of DCPR-2034 but notified on 13.11.2018

6. Increase in premiums, etc. due to linkage with ready reckoner

7. Demonetisation affecting the purchasing power of the people

2017:

1. Roll out of new system GST leading to mismatch in agreed contract pricing

2. Enactment of RERA provisions on Ongoing projects

2018:

1. The collapse of IL&FS and its negative impact on NBFCs

2. Action in scams of HDIL, DHFL, PMC Bank, Yes Bank

2019:

1. Delay in implementation of DCPR-2034

2. Delay in implementation of instalment facility

2020:

1. Imposition of lockdowns from March 2020

2. Financial crisis

3. Labour crisis

Other Reasons:

- Disputes in the land title

- Disputes between the landlord and developers

- Disputes with Investors or Creditors

- Litigation in various different forums/courts

- Attachment of the property/project by ED, EOW, Tax or other authorities

Chapter 3

Effects of Increasing number of Stalled Projects

Increasing number of stalled projects can have some bad effects on other sectors, companies and stakeholders, some of them have been enumerated below:

- Loss of confidence amongst prospective buyers

- Financial Institution's safe approach to lending terms

- A lot of funds getting stuck in the project

- Evaporation of Investor mechanism, which was parallel funding to the promoter

- Lack of promotional activities by various regulators in the field of real estate

- Slowdown in employment, migration of labour etc., as Real estate industry is one of the biggest employers of labour in India

- This also has a cascading effect in other industries and sectors which depend on real estate sector or provide inputs or raw materials for Real estate projects such as cement, steel, paint, etc.

- This can have a cascading effect on the Indian GDP and Indian Economy as a whole. Real estate industry contributes almost 7% to India's GDP, a slowdown in the sector due to stuck projects is most likely to have an effect on the economy

Chapter 4

Stalled Real Estate projects: A look at the ground situation

It is a common perception that all housing sectors falter under pressure from delayed projects. However, data shows that the total number of residential units classified as delayed/stalled in the top seven cities stands at 4.54 lakhs as of 2019

About 84% of these units existed in the two major cities: Delhi NCR (62%) and Mumbai (22%). These two cities have always been on the investors' radar due to the promising benefits and scope of expansion they offer. To top it off, looking at five years since the launch of the project, evaluating delayed/stalled residential projects - i.e. residential projects launched before or before 2014 and under construction, referred delayed/stalled projects and a total number of flats/flats for these projects identified as stalled/delayed residential units.

Contrary to the common myth that every segment of residential property is concerned, it is medium income and premium real estate projects that are very delayed.

City-wise analysis of stalled housing projects

City	No of delayed/stalled residential units	Share of overall delayed/stalled residential units
Bengaluru	28,400	6.3%
Chennai	8,500	1.9%
Delhi NCR	2,81,000	61.8%
Hyderabad	2,400	0.5%
Kolkata	17,800	3.9%
Mumbai	99,900	22.0%
Pune	16,400	3.6%
India	4,54,000	100%

Source: (JLL Research, 2019)

There is a general panic in the market, due to the failure of IL&FS, DHFL, etc., and this has led to many projects being reported as being stalled by the media due to financial concerns. This has led many brokers to avoid such projects altogether, and the media has reported a much larger amount than was seen earlier.

Overview of Stalled Projects in India

Stalled Project Scenario in 2019:

Projects get slowed down because of three significant reasons – endorsements not got, financing not got, or deals not up to the extended imprint. It is a typical discernment that the whole private area is reeling under the weight of postponed ventures. In any case, information shows that the all-out number of private units delegated deferred/slowed down, in the best seven refers to, remains at 4.54 lakhs. Practically 84% of these units were available in two significant metro urban communities: Delhi NCR (62%) and Mumbai (22%).

These two urban areas had consistently been on the radar of financial specialists because of the promising returns and the extension for development that they advertised. To show up the information, thought about a time a long time from the dispatch of the venture to assess the postponed/slowed down private undertakings – for example, private projects dispatched at the very latest in 2014 and still under development have been alluded to as deferred/slowed down activities, and the complete number of pads/lofts in these ventures are arranged as postponed/slowed down private units.

Analysis of stalled housing projects:

There is an overall frenzy on the lookout because of the disappointment of IL&FS, DHFL, and so forth. This has brought about a few ventures being accounted for as slowed down by the media over financing concerns. This has prompted a few specialists to maintain a strategic distance from such ventures inside and out, and the media reveals a more considerable number than watched. The issue is additionally misrepresented by agents, who are not getting commissions from even great manufacturers because of liquidity limitations.

The Supreme Court's milestone Verdict on Amrapali Developers has revived the expectations of lakhs of home purchasers who have been standing by uselessly to convey their homes. While comparative improvements concerning other stuck undertakings are anticipated, the pinnacle court has now started a trend with a resonating message - agree or die.

As indicated by research, upwards of 220 ventures rising to 1.74 lakh homes, are slowed down in the best seven urban areas alone. Dispatched either in 2013 or previously, these ventures have no development movement going on. The general estimation of all slowed down units is assessed to be more than Rs 1,77,400 crore. The more significant part of these ventures has been grounded due to either liquidity issues or prosecution. Practically 66% of these slowed down units have just been offered to purchasers who have been abandoned – helpless. The net assessed estimation of these sold units is around Rs 111,100 crore.

Of these business sectors, the National Capital Region (NCR) market has the most significant heap up of slowed down units with 1.18 lakh homes or 68% of the absolute stuck stock spread over more than 67 ventures with a general estimation of Rs 82,200 crore. Of this, almost 69% or 83,470 units are now sold out. Around 98% of NCR's stuck ventures are situated in Noida and Greater Noida alone, while different urban communities like Gurugram and Ghaziabad have insignificant stock.

The Mumbai Metropolitan Region (MMR) follows next, with almost 38,060 units slowed down over the city. In any case, the quantity of stuck units in this district is higher than in NCR. MMR's slowed down the unit's length more than 89 ventures as against 67 ventures in NCR. Strangely, regarding estimation of the slowed-down units, MMR is very near NCR, with slowed down units worth over Rs 80,200 crore as against Rs 82,200 crore in NCR. Despite a massive parity in the overall number of stalled units between the two major regions, MMR's astronomical property prices have kept this difference minimal.

Pune comes next with almost 28 ventures containing 9,650 units worth Rs 7,000 crore slowed down, trailed by Hyderabad with almost 4,150 units worth Rs 3,600 crore stuck. Bengaluru has 26 ventures, including 3,870 stuck units worth Rs 4,200 crore. With so many projects stuck across the top cities, affected home buyers now see a glimmer of hope with the Supreme Court's intervention in the Amrapali case.

Stalled Project Scenario in 2020

During delayed lockdown and proceeded with vulnerabilities concerning a re-visitation of some routineness, usage of undertakings worth Rs 9.9 lakh crore was slowed down during the initial nine months of 2020 till September 30, as per a most recent report by industry think tank Center for Monitoring Indian Economy (CMIE). The report, in any case, said that ventures worth Rs 9.2 lakh crore were restored during a similar period.

CMIE's Capex administration, which tracks the inception, usage and finishing of limit extending ventures, had announced toward the beginning of July this year that 674 projects worth Rs 9.7 lakh crore were slowed down due to the lockdown during the January-March quarter. These were transcendently in March. The examination by the CMIE demonstrated that another eight undertakings worth Rs 6,200 crore were slowed down in the April-June quarter of the current financial.

These numbers presently stand overhauled at 721 undertakings worth Rs 9.8 lakh crore in the March 2020 quarter and 22 ventures worth Rs 8,500 in the June 2020 quarter. Another Rs 3,200 worth of ventures were slowed down in the quarter finished September 2020," The business think tank said that vast numbers of these undertakings, whose execution was slowed down, continued exercises as the seriousness of the lockdown was downsized dynamically.

The investigation demonstrated that around Rs 4,100 crore worth of projects whose usage was slowed down were relinquished during the initial nine months of 2020. Not long before the lockdown, this arrived at the midpoint of over Rs 10,000 crore and before substantially more.

In the wake of COVID-19 driving cross country lockdown and work interruption brought about by this, Indian organisations avoided finishing limit extension venture ventures they had started previously. Adding to it, waiting for vulnerabilities about a popular recovery will incur delays in venture finishing plans. New venture declarations tumble to Rs 58,689 crore in the September quarter

When the lockdown started at first, ventures got slowed down amazingly; however, the vast majority of them continued work as the lockdown was facilitated. The net impact on slowing down has been minor; however, the effect on venture fruitions has been unmistakably more extreme.

Activities worth Rs 32,600 crore were charged during the quarter finished September 2020. This is the second continuous quarter when venture culminations have tumbled to such sharply low levels. In the June 2020 quarter, ventures worth Rs 24,000 crore were finished. In correlation, venture fruitions found the median value of Rs 1.3 lakh crore per quarter in 2019-20 and Rs 1.6 lakh crore per quarter in 2018-19.

Numerous financial pointers that had fallen pointedly during the June quarter of the current monetary indicated a significant yet fragmented recovery in the September quarter. Project consummations, be that as it may, demonstrated no improvement, while the pace of venture finish dropped forcefully during the lockdown.

This rate, which estimates ventures finished communicated as a per cent of estimation of activities under usage, dropped to 0.2 per cent in the June quarter, while it recouped insignificantly to 0.28 per cent in the September quarter. These extents contrast inadequately, and the average pace of culmination of well more than 1 per cent in the ongoing past, the examination appeared. Most activities finished in the September quarter were in the foundation areas. Rail and street transport asserted the most excellent offer among all areas, with these two together representing 43 per cent of the all-out culmination of activities. Thirty-five per cent of the complete estimation of charged activities was in the vehicle framework administration areas, the CMIE study appeared.

According to the CMIE study, government ventures established 63 per cent of all dispatching of activities in the September quarter. In the last seventy-five per cent, government ventures have represented more than 60% of all appointed, while the private area has made a more modest commitment to fruition.

(Source: JLL, Anarock)

Chapter 6

Promoter Definition as per RERA

Promoter is:-

1. a person who constructs or causes to be constructed an independent building or a building consisting of flats, or converts an existing building or a part thereof into flats including the redevelopment of building or buildings, for the purpose of selling all or some of the flats to other persons and includes his assignees; or

2. a person who develops land into a project, whether or not the person also constructs structures on any of the plots, for the purpose of selling to other persons all or some of the plots in the said project, whether with or without structures thereon; or

3. any development authority or any other public body in respect of allottees of, -

    •   buildings or flats, as the case may be, constructed by such authority or body on lands owned by it or placed at its disposal by the Government; or

    •   plots owned by such authority or body or placed at its disposal by the Government, for the purpose of selling all or some of the flats or plots; or

4. an apex State level co-operative housing finance society and a primary cooperative housing society which constructs flats or

buildings for its Members or in respect of the allottees of such flats or buildings; or

5.   any other person who acts himself as a builder, coloniser, contractor, developer, estate developer or by any other name or claims to be acting as the holder of a power of attorney from the owner of the land on which the building or flat is constructed or plot is developed for sale; or

(Source: RERA,2016)

It is to be noted that under Self Redevelopment and incase of stalled projects when society terminates the agreement of the non-performing developer, such society becomes "Promoter" as per recent judgements of Honorable Bombay High Court.

Chapter 7

Remedy for Home Buyers

In this situation, what should home buyers do?

Before buying a property, buyers should check the RERA website for sales details, approval status, and construction status. They should also consider the banks or NBFC financing the project.

Looking at a builder's record can help to some extent, but one should not rely solely on it. The financial position of the developer could deteriorate rapidly if funding is shortened. In this situation, the property consultant's role becomes critical because they can help the home buyer identify the right seller and avoid them by getting involved in such a risky project.

Project delays in the residential segment are not a pan-India phenomenon and are only limited to the major metropolitan cities of Delhi NCR and Mumbai, in terms of quantum, as well as the value of projects.

Secondly, the slowdown in completing projects is not across the entire spectrum of housing categories but is significantly visible in the upper-mid and premium categories. What is needed is perhaps a push from the government and funding agencies, along with a strict code of conduct among developers, to improve the situation

Chapter 8

Strategies to Revive Stalled Projects

With numerous land ventures slowed down or deferred because of future legal disputes, land procurement issues, and buyer objections, developers receive new procedures to mix life into these undertakings.

Deferred and slowed down activities have impacted India's real estate market. Around 30% of 25 lakh properties dispatched during 2008-2014 have been deferred. Because of reliable weight from purchasers and forthcoming RERA guidelines, most developers are optimising the development work to complete their projects on schedule. Authorities think that ideal fruition ventures are a success win circumstance for the two purchasers just as developers.

By finishing their Projects on schedule, developers can restore the buyer certainty. In the current market, where private deals are generally moderate, developers with a great history of finish and quality have the purchasers' inclination.

Developers are adopting various strategies to revive their projects. For example, a developer in Noida is tying up with outsider contract-based workers to finish part-fabricated pinnacles in vast numbers of its projects where work had been slowed down because of a money crunch and court case. In this arrangement, a contractual worker would take up 4-5 towers and put forthright cash of his own to restore the work and take it to a phase where development-linked client instalments can be looked at.

A Mumbai-based mid-sized builder is currently in talks with a bigger, more established brand about becoming a joint venture partner in its under-construction suburban project. While JVs in real estate are typically formed for greenfield projects, the builder, in this case, has already completed 15 stories but is facing a sales challenge, according to Economic Times.

Above are some examples of how developers find different ways to revive the stalled project; we will further examine various strategies.

Joint Venture:

JVs are practically on the ascent in the Indian real estate market. While this training is more usual in new activities, the pattern can likewise be seen in stalled projects.

A joint venture is an association between numerous parties to co-operate and solidify their assets to develop a project. The more significant part of real estate ventures' vast scope is financed and overseen through a JV.

In India, non-finish projects have pushed real estate administrators (people with experience in executing a project) to work with real estate capital suppliers (Capital speculators).

What are the advantages of a joint Venture?

Principally, a JV benefits small scale developers. Solidification and consolidation with the Grade-A developers encourage little developers to convey great undertakings. Small scale developers probably won't approach a showcasing methodology or capital of that scale. A JV permits them to channelise their energies and adventure into ventures which are not in their degree without any help.

Then again, settled land developers could tweak their venture conveyance potential. It even ingrains trust in wary homebuyers as the name of a setup developer gets connected to the project. Primarily, a JV benefits small scale developers. Union and consolidation with the Grade-A developers encourage little developers to convey excellent undertakings. Small scale developers probably won't approach an advertising technique or capital of that scale. A JV permits them to channelise their energies and adventure into ventures which are not in their extension without any assistance.

Then again, settled real estate developer could calibrate their project conveyance potential. It even imparts trust in doubtful homebuyers as a setup developer's name gets connected to the undertaking.

What provoked the pattern of Joint Ventures in the real estate market?

The entry of the Real Estate (Regulation and Development) Act, 2016 and the Real Estate Regulatory Authority's ensuing arrangement brought straightforwardness and responsibility into the land area. Notwithstanding, the administrative system didn't go down well with little league developers who couldn't conform to the strict standards. The individuals who couldn't endure went into insolvency. The individuals who needed to endure framed joint Ventures with large developers.

The law has imparted straightforwardness and has supported unfamiliar, just as institutional interest in the area. It has additionally helped the area shed its questionable qualification of being sloppy.

The tie-up with third parties:

With numerous developers confronting a budgetary crunch, they have now tied up with outsiders, for example, development and planner firms, to complete their undertakings. For example, Amrapali Group has tied up with around ten contractual workers to complete around 50 towers in the entirety of their projects in Noida. The contractual workers will put their cash forthright and get the instalments once the gathering looks for an instalment through the development connected arrangement.

This strategy is widely used in the market. Nowadays, many developers are using this strategy as an example of Noida given above. The developer ties up with the contracting firm due to low working capital as RERA in the picture developer has to complete the project in stipulated time.

Selling projects to other developers:

Incapable of taking forward the development of their project because of money related crunch, developers are auctioning off their territory or undertakings to different developers hanging tight for an occasion to set their foot on the lookout. A portion of the models incorporates SNN Builders buying under-development venture in Hebbal, Bangalore from Essar Group and Kanakia Group getting land bundle from Windsor Realty in Kanjurmarg, Mumbai.

Property swap strategies, such as the one used in NCR, are also used by developers. According to the Economic Times, cash-strapped real estate developers in the National Capital Region offer property-swap schemes to homebuyers stuck in stalled projects, giving them the option to switch to another property if they are willing to pay at least 70% of the price of the new property.

Partnering with the other party is also not easy; as per RERA developer has to consent from existing buyers to appoint a new party or sell the project.

Authorities and consumers are also coming up with ideas.

Not just developers, clients, and authorities are also coming out with imaginative plans to help developers meet their objectives. As of late, homebuyers in NCR have begun indicating backing to developers to get their activities given throughout on time instead of hauling them to courts. Activities, for example, having a delegate of purchasers on the administration board, have been taken well both by developers and home purchasers.

The authorities have additionally begun contributing. The Noida Authority has planned to permit enlistment of pads on a master rata premise wherein developers can somewhat clear their levy, and enrolments would be permitted from the expert for an equal number of properties as coordinated. Prior enrolments were not permitted till the developer cleared every one of his duty.

Chapter 9

Government Initiatives

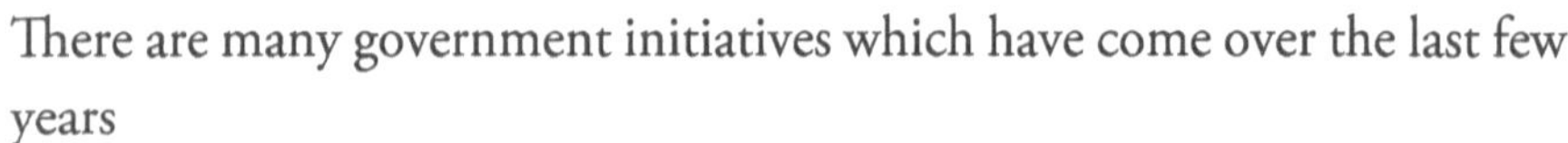

There are many government initiatives which have come over the last few years

- Central Government Initiatives

  1. RERA

  2. NCLT

  3. SWAMIH Fund

We will discuss all of these in detail in the coming chapters

- Maharashtra Government Initiatives:

1. SRA Amnesty Scheme:

   In order to push the stalled 380 SRA projects in the city, the state government has cleared the Slum Rehabilitation Authority's (SRA) Amnesty Scheme. Under the scheme, Financial Institutions which have lent to such projects will be admitted as co-developers and will be able to get easier clearances to restart the project. It is estimated that the Financial Institutions have invested over Rs 35,000 crore in these projects which will now free up.

   The government, on its part, has allotted 520 such stalled slum projects to new developers, all these projects have been stuck for last 10-15 years, this step will give relief to 40,000 families.

These 520 slum projects were stuck due to unscrupulous developers and other reasons; hence the government cancelled the letter of intent given for these 520 slums and will be appointing new developers in place of them.

There are around 2,131 SRA projects ongoing as of March 2022, out of which approximately 533 projects have been stuck since 2005. Most of these projects are from the following wards of the BMC:

- 49 projects in the R-South ward (Kandivali)
- 50 projects in the P-North ward (Malad)
- 53 projects in the P-South ward (Goregaon)
- 63 projects in the S ward (Bhandup and Powai)
- 104 projects in the M-East ward (Govandi, Mankhurd)

2. Cess Building Redevelopment Policy:

The Mumbai Building Repairs and Reconstruction Board (MBRRB), an undertaking of MHADA, has amended the redevelopment scheme, which was approved by Maharashtra Government in September 2020, the policy will help expedite and restart the development of stuck and abandoned Cess Buildings in the city

Figure 32: Cess Building

According to the newly amended act, MHADA can now acquire the property with just 51% occupant consent as opposed to 71% earlier. This policy will apply to cess buildings present in South Mumbai and in which MHADA is the custodian.

Chapter 10

Role of RERA

Take-over of the project under RERA Laws – RERA is a new set of laws that were enacted to promote the real estate industry and to protect the homebuyers. As per section 8 of the RERA Act, the RERA authority has the power to cancel the registration of any project and, with the prior permission of the respective State Govt. can take over the project. However, there have been very few instances where such power of take-over has been exercised.

The following are the benefit and challenge analysis:

Benefits:

- Filing the complaint with the RERA authority is easy

- May be joined by other homebuyers

- Local supervision

Challenges:

- 2/3 of allottees are required to initiate such a take-over process

- Prior approval from State Govt is required

- No prescribed mechanism to take over and complete the pending construction work

- It is very difficult join by 2/3 of allottees to form an association for this purpose

- Non-involvement by Banks and other creditors

- Overriding effect of IBC Laws, if any IBC petition is filed by any other creditor, the process would be stopped

- The legal right of assets and management lies with old management

- No moratorium on other legal remedies and recoveries, i.e. the DRT may initiate the sell the property for the banks

- Non-cooperation by banks, old management or other creditors

- No legal structure for distribution of money etc.

Chapter 11

Role of NCLT and IBC

Resolution Process by NCLT under IBC Laws– This is the most secure, practical, and result-oriented process. As per IBC Laws, if any company is unable to pay its debts or, in the case of homebuyers, unable to handover the units as per the Builder Buyer Agreement (BBA), then Hon'ble NCLT (National Company Law Tribunal) may initiate the Resolution process upon filing the petition u/s 7 or 9 of Insolvency and Bankruptcy Code, 2016 (IBC Laws). There have been various cases where real estate company has been resolved or are being resolved under IBC Laws.

Under IBC Laws, in the case of homebuyers, 10% of allottees or 100 buyers, whichever is less, may file a petition u/s 7 of IBC Laws before Hon'ble NCLT to initiate the resolution process. If NCLT is convinced that default has occurred and the application is complete in all aspects, the CIRP (Corporate Insolvency Resolution Process) is initiated. The following are the benefit and challenge analysis:

Benefits:

- Due to Moratorium u/s 14 of IBC Laws, all rights and power vest at one place to find a resolution

- Overriding effect – IBC Laws has an overriding effect on other laws in India, be it RERA, Consumer Court, Civil Courts, and other Courts & Authority

- Builder has to give all its assets and liabilities to the IRP/RP

- NCLT appointed IRP, to take care of management and business

- The committee of Creditors (body of financial Creditors) takes all decisions regarding the resolution process

- Timebound process for resolution Plan

- Participation by all Creditors

- Supervision of process by IRP, IBBI, NCLT

- Open bid to get maximization of assets

- Timebound prescribed process to be followed for resolution

- Only NCLT, then appeal before Hon'ble NCLAT and Hon'ble Supreme Court power to deal with matters

- RP is appointed as per Committee of Creditors (CoC) approval

Challenges:

- Filing petitions by more than 10% or 100 homebuyers before Hon'ble NCLT

- Lack of knowledge of IBC Laws

- Most IRP don't take out of box solutions to give maximum value

The resolution process is based on the "Creditor-in-Charge" principle. Hence, if the builder is unable to complete the project, the fate of the company shall be decided by the creditors (Financial Creditors)

Chapter 12

NCLT or RERA?

If we talk about a more effective legal remedy before homebuyers, then approaching NCLT is anyway a better option available to them. It has more effective outcomes as compared to that RERA. RERA undoubtedly is a law, particularly dealing with the real estate concern, but the execution of RERA orders is still a big question before the system. But even after knowing this fact, buyers approach RERA because the RERA Authorities entertain individual complaints.

Since the IBC Laws have an overriding effect and have the legal framework of the complete resolution process, the IBC process through NCLT is more effective, timebound, practical, and result-oriented.

The right legal remedy comes from the right legal advice. Getting a good legal team that shows you the right legal path is half battle won. Getting delayed justice is no justice. A good legal team will help you in getting justice on time with an effective remedy.

Chapter 13

SWAMIH Fund

Special Window for completion of construction of Affordable and Mid-Income Housing Projects also known as SWAMIH FUND

What is SWAMIH Fund?

In November 2019, the central Government launched the 'Special Window for Funding Stalled Affordable and Middle-Income Housing Projects' or 'SWAMIH' Scheme. The objective of the scheme is to provide priority debt financing for the completion of stalled housing projects falling under the affordable and middle-income housing categories. This 'last mile financing' of stalled projects will be extended through a Category-II AIF (Alternate Investment Fund) debt fund registered with the Securities and Exchange Board of India (SEBI).

SWAMIH Fund acts as a "virtual CFOs for the project" and is not a lender borrower relationship.

In terms of collateral benefits, he said that construction sites have the highest labour density. Also, developers with significant repute, developers who are going through stress in a particular project and who could not start or develop other land banks or other projects because of negatively which has come from a single project, can now approach SWAMIH and get that situation resolved and launch other projects.

Why was the SWAMIH fund needed?

The central Government, in a Press Information Bureau release, stated that the SWAMIH fund was launched to provide relief to real estate developers that require funding to complete their unfinished projects and consequently ensure the timely delivery of homes to the home-buyers. It is expected that the scheme will aid the growth of the real estate sector in India. About 1,509 housing projects comprising approximately 4.58 lakh housing units which have been stuck fulfil the eligibility criteria listed below to benefit from the scheme.

For whom has the fund been conceptualized?

The real estate projects seeking last-mile funding from SWAMIH must be RERA-registered projects which have been stalled due to a lack of adequate funds. They must also fall under the 'Affordable and Middle Income Project' category. Net-worth positive projects are also eligible for SWAMIH funding. Finally, each of these projects must be very close to completion. Net-worth positive projects are those projects for which the value of their receivables (debts owed to them by buyers), plus the value of their unsold inventories is greater than their completion costs and outstanding liabilities.

The Government has defined an 'affordable and middle-income projects' as those projects in which the flats do not measure more than 200 square metres in carpet area and are priced as below:

- Upto INR 2 crore in the Mumbai Metropolitan Region

- Upto INR 1.5 crore in the National Capital Region, Chennai, Kolkata, Pune, Hyderabad, Bangalore and Ahmedabad

- Upto INR 1 crore in the rest of India

Fund Manager:

SBICAP Ventures Limited will be the Investment Manager of the SWAMIH fund. The role of the Investment Manager will be to undertake fund-raising, carrying out investments and manage the fund team

Investors:

The Central Government, through the Department of Economic Affairs, is the sponsor of the SWAMIH fund. It has infused INR 10,000 crore in the Fund. The Government seeks to obtain matching contributions from other investors including sovereign wealth funds, domestic pension and provident funds, global pension funds, banks, NBFCs and other institutional investors, to generate a total corpus of INR 25,000 crore.

Progress of the fund disbursal till now:

SWAMIH Fund will invest ₹24,151 crore across 252 stalled projects

According to a government statement, around 111 projects have been granted final approval. Investments (deal size) will be ₹10,992 crore, against which the project cost is ₹30,503 crore. Beneficiaries or total units under the investment will be 63,716.

On the other hand, preliminary approval has already been granted for 142 projects, entailing an investment of ₹13,159 crore, where the project cost was ₹36,267 crore, and the number of dwelling units coming up stood at 83,662.

The Fund made its first successful exit in October 2021, the project, which was in Borivali, Mumbai, the Rivali Park residential project was the first to receive funding under the SWAMIH Fund. CCI projects pvt ltd was developing the project

Funding Eligibility:

For projects to be eligible for support from the alternative investment debt fund, the Government clarified the 'positive net worth' condition. The Fund will not offer support to ventures that the National Company Law Tribunal (NCLT) heard in the Supreme Court and high courts but will take up others.

The cabinet approved the plan to revitalise the ailing industry, which is expected to provide relief to homebuyers, create jobs, increase cement and steel sales, and boost the economy. Net worth positive denotes that the value of receivables plus unsold inventory should be higher than the project's completion cost and outstanding liabilities.

The eligibility criteria to receive funding from Alternative Investments Funds (AIF) is mentioned below:

- Projects that are RERA-registered:

  - Firstly, the project must be registered with the state real estate regulatory authority.

  - Projects meant for middle and low-income groups.

  - The window is intended for mid to low-budget homes only. For this reason, the unit price limit for the Mumbai market was maintained at up to Rs 2 crores, up to Rs 1.5 crores for the National Capital Area, Pune, Chennai, Hyderabad, Kolkata, Ahmedabad and Bengaluru and up to Rs 1 crore for the rest of the world. For the same reason, the carpet area per unit has been limited to 200 square metres.

- Projects that are net-worth positive:

  - The project must be positive in terms of net worth. This ensures that the cost of completion and the accrued liabilities of these projects do not surpass the receivables' value in these projects and the inventory of the unsold ones. Projects stuck with solvency problems in the National Company Law Tribunal or have been considered nonperforming assets can also seek funds if they happen to be positive in net worth.

- Projects with no litigation:

  - However, projects that are trapped in the high court or supreme court proceedings will not be considered under the AIF.

- Projects close to completion:

  - The government memorandum also states that it should be 'very near' to complete a project to obtain funds. It also states that only those projects where a lack of capital causes the delay will be given liquidity.

- Fund Structure:

  - The Government will serve as the proposed Fund's sponsor and has pledged Rs 10,000 crore. As the investment manager, SBICAP Ventures Ltd will be involved and responsible for fundraising, investments and the fund team's management. In addition to Life Insurance Corporation of India (LIC) and others, the Fund is looking for matching contributions from lenders such as State Bank of India to build a corpus of around Rs 25,000 crore.

  - The Fund will oversee the disbursement of capital and track projects' execution directly or through third-party providers by the developer. As part of the sanction process, current lenders will be consulted. The investment manager will perform a thorough analysis, including feedback given by external due diligence agencies.

  - This control process would be part of the developers' contractual agreement. Disbursements will occur only after the completion of documentation.

  - The Fund expects its assets to be predominantly structured in the form of non-convertible debentures, subject to legal, regulatory or other considerations. The investment manager would assess the returns based on each project's risk profile and details, it said. To determine whether the proposal meets the Fund's investment criteria, the investment manager will conduct an internal financial review, which will be supplemented by external due diligence agencies covering areas such as title, financials, real estate, and legal, among others, as well as consultation with existing lenders. The collection of projects and developers will be responsible for the Fund's investment manager and investment committee.

- The financial objectivity of the mechanism will not intervene with investors, including the Government, "he said, adding that the fund's investment objectives will drive the decision."

Special Window:

The Union Cabinet, chaired over by Prime Minister, approved the creation of a "Special Window" fund to provide priority debt financing to complete stalled housing projects in the affordable and middle-income housing sectors.

The Government acts as the Fund's sponsor, and the Government's total pledge to be infused will be up to INR 10,000 crore. The Fund will be professionally managed and set up as a Category-II AIF (Alternate Investment Fund) debt fund registered with SEBI.

It is suggested that SBICAP Ventures Limited be hired as the Investment Manager for the first AIF under the Special Window.

In turn, this Fund will offer relief to developers who need financing to complete a set of unfinished projects and ensure that home buyers are supplied with homes.

Since the real estate industry is fundamentally connected to a range of other industries, growth in this sector would also positively impact stress relief in other major sectors of the Indian economy.

The unique window's emphasis would be on projects that are delayed because of the lack of funding for construction, it said. Projects where the restructuring plan has not been accepted or rejected by the committee of creditors under the insolvency resolution procedure will not be considered.

The "very close to completion" projects would have priority, it said. The Fund does not accept ventures that require fraud or diversion. As per average risk, there will be caps at the project, developer and city levels.

With the Government providing monetary support through its alternative investment fund to as many as 33 housing projects, over 25,000 stuck housing units will likely be completed soon. According to finance minister, a Rs 4,197 crore investment has received final approval through Special Window for Affordable and Mid-Income Housing (SWAMIH) fund. The FM said this Fund would contribute to the construction of 25,048 housing units in a tweet on October 8, 2020.

The Fund was formed in November 2019 to assist RERA-registered stuck projects in India's major housing markets after obtaining approval from the union cabinet. The Fund's monetary support will result in over 60,000 units being built across prime residential markets, including the Metropolitan Area of Mumbai, Chennai, Bengaluru, the National Capital Region and Pune. The SWAMIH fund will also provide liquidity to pending housing projects in Maharashtra, Chandigarh, Uttar Pradesh, Haryana, and Rajasthan.

Loan Restructuring:

Retail loans issued to consumers in qualifying stalled projects will be restructured by Reserve Bank of India (RBI) guidelines and bank board-approved policies.

"Since the real estate industry is fundamentally related to a range of other industries, growth in this sector would also have a positive impact on stress relief in other major sectors of the Indian economy," the Government said.

To get through the current situation, cash flow planning and debt commitment structuring are critical. This would include the drawing up of a crisis management strategy and cash situation stress testing. Close project monitoring, post-moratorium options discussion with lenders and exploration of rescue/revival capital for stressed projects will also be required.

Investment Committee:

An investment committee makes the SWAMIH Fund's investment and divestment decisions ("IC"). The IC is made up of SVL team members as well as independent members. The IC must always have a minimum of four members and a maximum of seven members. Investment proposals submitted on behalf of the Fund are forwarded to the IC for final approval. The IC makes investment decisions unanimously. The Investment Manager may alter, replace, or reassemble the IC members (except the CIO).

Advisory Board:

The Investment Manager has formed an advisory board comprised of investor representatives (the "Advisory Board"). As a Contributor, the Government of India is entitled to up to two seats on the Advisory Board, which will be available to one nominee from each of the (i) Department of Economic Affairs, and (ii) the Department of Financial Services, under the Ministry of Finance, Government of India. Other Contributors who have made a Capital Commitment to the Fund each have one seat on the Advisory Board.

The Advisory Board shall:

- Examine potential conflicts of interest and approve or disapprove of them. If the Advisory Board does not give the Fund its permission to invest, the Fund will not be permitted to make such an investment.

- Examine and approve the interim and permanent CIO appointments.

- Provide any advice requested by the Investment Manager.

List of projects:

SWAMIH Investment Fund I has so far approved Rs 8,767 crore for 81 stressed residential projects, according to Finance Minister

Finance Minister was discussing the Special Window's performance for Affordable and Mid-Income Housing (SWAMIH) with finance secretaries and senior management teams from the State Bank of India, SBI Capital Markets, and SBICAPS Ventures (SVL).

The approved Fund would allow the construction of nearly 60,000 homes across India. These projects are spread across a variety of markets, including big cities like the National Capital Region (NCR), Mumbai Metropolitan Region (MMR), Bengaluru, Chennai, and Pune, as well as tier-II cities like Karnal, Panipat, Lucknow, Surat, Dehradun, Kota, Nashik, Chandigarh, Vizag, Nagpur and Jaipur,

Among these projects, 18 have received final approval, and disbursement is in different phases across seven residential projects.

List of Cleared Projects as of June 2022

List of Final clearance Projects

Sr. No.	Developer	Project	Location
1	Mantri Developers	Mantri Serenity	Bengaluru
2	CCI Projects Ltd	Rivali Park	Borivali, MMR
3	Ramprashtha Group	Primera	Gurgaon, Sector 37D, NCR
4	Naman Group	Naman Premier	Andheri (E), Mumbai, MMR
5	Essel	Asha Bahadurgarh	Bahadurgarh, NCR
6	TDI	Lake Grove	Kundli, Sonipat, NCR
7	Lodha	Upper Thane	Thane , MMR
8	Sikka	Kimaya Greens	Dehradun
9	Urban Land	Amangani Peaceful Homes	Rewari, Haryana
10	Plaza	Elite Acres	OMR, Chennai
11	Ansal Housing	Highland Park	Sector 103, Gurgaon
12	Vayuputra	Gem Paradise	Andheri (W), Mumbai, MMR
13	Ozone	WF8	Whitefield, Bengaluru
14	Magnus	Vedantam Minaret	Indirapuram, NCR
15	Vilasa	Taruchaya Residency	Ajmer Road, Jaipur
16	Moongipa	Windspace Amelio	DN Nagar, MMR
17	Playtor	Playtor Ranjangaon	Ranjangaon, Pune
18	SS Group	Leaf	New Gurgaon, Haryana, NCR

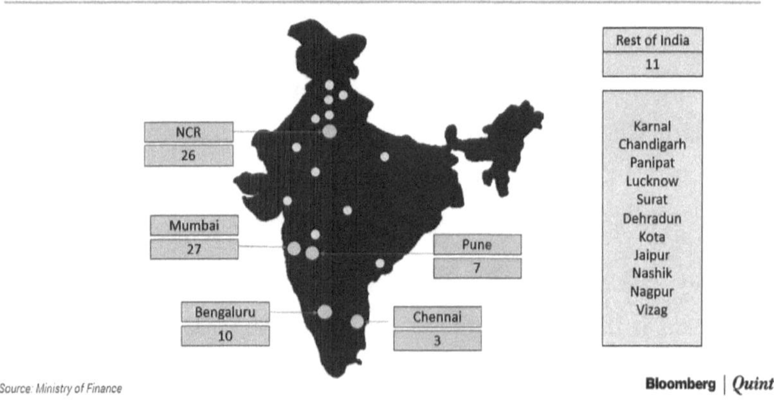

As of 2023, SWAMIH Fund has completed 20,557 homes since inception in 2019. The fund has helped in completing construction in 26 projects while unlocking liquidity of more than Rs 35,000 crores

Fund targets to complete over 81,000 homes in next 3 years, i.e by 2026 across 30 Tier 1 and Tier 2 cities in India.

As of 2023, SWAMIH fund had so far provided final approval to about 130 projects with sanctions worth over Rs 12,000 crore

As of 2024, SWAMIH Fund has had resounding success in the past few years since its inception, it has come as a relief to all the stakeholders in the industry. The last mile gap has helped in:

- Revival of the project

- Completion of the construction of houses, successful possession to buyer

- Payment of pending dues to creditors

- Reducing the overall bad debts and loans in the industry

- Instilling confidence in the buyers and improving the sentiment

- Aiding in overall growth of Real estate and related industry

Following are the successful project resolutions/revivals that SWAMIH fund has helped in:

- Amrapali group

- Rivali Park

- Asset Precious

- Lodha Upper Thane

- Pyramid Urban

- Gem Paradise

- SS Leaf

- Elite Acres

- MK Gabino

- Zen Residences

- The Marquise
- Newa Bhakti Park
- Naman Premier
- Paranjpe Blueridge

Among many others

(Source: sbiventures.co.in)

Chapter 14

Bad Bank

National Asset Reconstruction Co. Ltd (NARCL) also envisioned as bad bank

What is a bad bank?

Seen as a panacea for India's massive bad loan problem, NARCL was set up on 7 July with an authorised capital of ₹100 crores and has been classified as a "Union government company".

Why was a bad bank needed?

The plan to form a bad bank to clean up banks' balance sheets was announced in the Union budget in February 2021

If a bank has high non-performing assets (NPAs), a large part of its profits would be utilised to cut losses. As a result, any bank with high NPAs is likely to become more risk averse and would be less willing to lend money to borrowers. It would become more difficult for businesses and consumers to take loans from banks, thereby impacting the overall robustness of the economy.

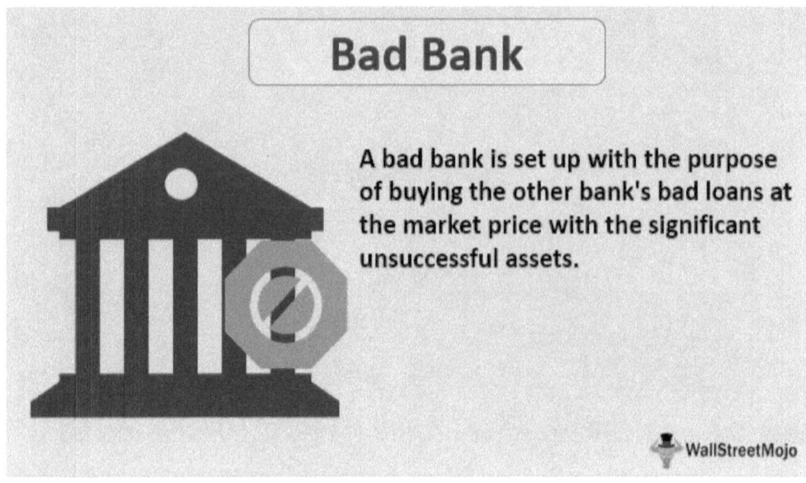

Moreover, in India, a large portion of NPAs is with the government-owned public sector banks. In the past, the government had to infuse fresh capital to improve the financial health of the PSBs. The government infusing fresh capital in PSB means less money for other schemes.

How was the bad bank formed?

It suffered from delays after the Reserve Bank of India said it was unhappy over the proposed structure. Lenders then presented a revised proposal to the regulator.

Under the new structure approved by the regulator, the bad bank—the National Asset Reconstruction Co. Ltd (NARCL)—will acquire and aggregate the bad loan accounts from banks, while India Debt Resolution Co. Ltd (IDRCL) will handle the resolution process under an exclusive arrangement.

A total of 38 accounts worth ₹82,845 crore have been identified for transfer to the NARCL. NARCL will identify and acquire assets on a 15:85 cash and security receipt (SR) basis. These SRs will be issued in favour of the transferring lenders and will be secured by a government guarantee for their face value.

While public sector banks have taken a majority stake in NARCL, IDRCL will be majority-owned by private sector banks.

There are global parallels to taking the bad bank route to clean up stressed assets. But an earlier bid by India to address non-performing assets issue had limited success when the government had set up the Stressed Asset Stabilization Fund (SASF) in 2004 to hive off the stressed assets of IDBI Ltd.

Key arguments in favour of establishing a Bad bank:

Bad banks are more complex and time consuming to set up but have benefits, both in terms of the core franchise and in terms of the non-core assets which are being worked out.

- Frees management bandwidth and specifically allows the management to:
    - Focus on driving the performance of the core business
    - Right-size the infrastructure for the organisation
    - Reduce the balance sheet and realise value from non-core assets through tailored solutions
    - Release capital into or lower the capital requirements at the core business
- Quicker resolution: Pooling of bad assets under a single entity can help in terms of resolutions (quicker decisions) as and when growth improves, and demand for these assets increase.
- Plugs in loopholes in the ARC model: Private-run ARCs have not seen much success in resolving bad debts. International experience shows that a professionally run central agency with government backing could overcome the coordination and political issues that have impeded progress over the past years.

- Domain expertise:

  - A dedicated Bad bank may be better than a number of PSU banks replicating similar departments in their respective organisations.

  - Under a competent management and Board, the value of these stressed assets could be better preserved.

  - Domain focus could potentially help tap long-term pools of foreign and domestic capital via equity/debt issuance versus

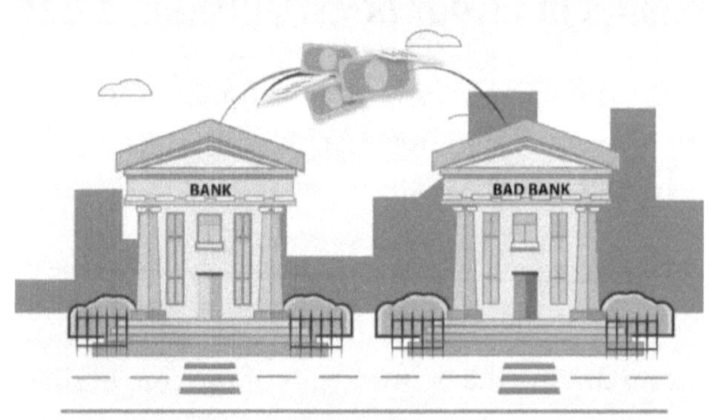

Figure 33: Concept of Bad Bank

Price Discovery: A Bad bank may be better suited to fix the appropriate prize:

- The transferring bank could make additional provisions in case the discovered cost is less than the book value, and the bank wants to retain the asset on its books.

- Capital relief: Based on the existing prudential norms as defined by the RBI, NPAs are still accounted for in the branch books, whereas the corresponding advances are also adjusted for provisions and write-offs to arrive at the Net Advances figure as published in the audited books of accounts.

Key arguments against establishing a Bad bank:

- Potential steep haircuts:

  A prominent issue with Bad banks is not the need for it, but how to set it up, particularly when debt and equity capital is scarce and costly and fair value of the assets under consideration is estimated to be low.

  Transfer at computed fair value with steep haircuts may cause a severe blow to the bottom line of the transferring bank, preventing a full transfer of risk to the Bad bank as contemplated

- Lack of buyer demand: The price at which toxic assets are to be transferred may not be market determined, and price discovery may not happen. A key challenge includes the need for rapid, reliable data collection and analysis:

  - Development of a detailed recovery/deleveraging plan

  - Design of a structure that meets capital objectives - Project based set up with cost base carefully aligned with asset recovery/deleveraging activity

    Developing and managing appropriate resources in areas such as restructuring and recovery, commercial real estate, IT and portfolio sales/M&A

    The need to utilise restructuring techniques for non-core assets when the

  - The workout unit itself has an intensive workload

  - The need for management to focus primarily on developing the core franchise (good bank) whilst appropriately managing the non-core assets

  Ownership disputes: Various options could be explored for the ownership of Bad banks – entirely government-backed funding, private funding, or a public-private partnership (PPP). While global Bad bank models with favourable outcomes were largely Government owned, many see the advantage in having a Bad bank owned by the banks collectively. This would ensure that when a bad loan is resolved, the profits will accrue to the owners, i.e. the banks themselves. This would make the loss they booked on selling the non-performing assets at a discount more palatable

Chapter 15

Slum Redevelopment

Slum Redevelopment in Mumbai has taken shape over the past few decades after the government of Maharashtra passed the Slum Rehabilitation Act, 1995. The act established the Slum Rehabilitation Authority (SRA).

The slum scheme has helped in rehabilitation of lakhs of residents in the Mumbai Metropolitan Region, but the scheme adoption has still been sluggish as more than a million residences are still to be constructed to make this a success. Mumbai Metropolitan Region alone demands an estimated 1.1 million affordable homes yet to be built

It has also been seen that many of these slum projects are stuck at various stages of development and are hence not able to clear of slums from city and provide a quality and respectable residences to these inhabitants.

In 2023, The Slum Rehabilitation Authority, in collaboration with the BMC and various special planning authorities, is set to revive ten slum redevelopment initiatives in Mumbai that have languished for 10-15 years.

The state housing department has issued a Government Resolution (GR) permitting the completion of stalled slum rehabilitation projects spanning Mumbai, Thane, and the Mumbai Metropolitan Region through partnerships with local self-government entities and specialised planning authorities such as MHADA, MMRDA, CIDCO, and others.

According to the GR, the financing for these projects will be entirely borne by the respective local self-government bodies or specialised planning authorities. Neither the SRA nor the state government will contribute funds to these endeavours. Valuation of existing construction will be conducted, and the local authority will reimburse the original builder. Both the rehabilitation and sale components of these projects will be undertaken by the local authorities. The units in the sale component will be made available in the open market under the government's 'Housing for All' initiative, with the proceeds from flat sales allocated to fund the project.

It is important to note that most of the stalled projects marked for transfer to the local bodies are situated on land owned by these entities. Nevertheless, a thorough assessment of the scheme's financial and technical feasibility will be carried out before handing it over to the local body, as stipulated in the GR.

(Source: constructionworld)

SWAMIH Fund I has also done a last mile funding of Rs 160 crore in a project by Stans Buildtech Homes located in Chembur

In order to revive the stalled slum redevelopment projects, the State Government of Maharashtra had also issued a Government Resolution dated 25th March 2022 ("GR") for implementation of the Amnesty Scheme thereby providing measures for reviving the stalled slum redevelopment projects in Mumbai. As per the housing department, there are about 380 slum rehabilitation projects stalled or turned dormant mainly due to financial, procedural and regulatory problems. These have been lying dormant since 2005

Following benefits and conditions have been provided under the GR:

- New developers will have to be appointed through tendering process for the slum redevelopment projects that are stalled due to non-appointment of developers or due lack of payment of rent to the slum dwellers. The approval of the general body of the committee of slum dwellers will not be needed for the appointment of new developers.

- The financial institutions (FIs) approved by the Reserve Bank of India (RBI) and the Securities Exchange Board of India (SEBI) would be allowed to complete rehabilitation projects.

- FIs that have already provided funds for the implementation of slum rehabilitation projects, will be notified as co-developers.

- RBI and SEBI-approved FIs will be exempted from the payment of 5 per cent premium.

- It will be mandatory for the developers/FIs to complete the rehabilitation portion under the Amnesty Scheme in a given time period. Besides, it will be compulsory for the new developers to regularly pay rent to slum dwellers.

- In the first year, the developers/FIs will have to complete 33% work and if delayed they will have to pay 1% of the land required for the construction of the saleable portion. They will have to complete 66% of the work in two years or pay a fine of 2% of the land required for the construction of the saleable portion. They will have to complete the scheme in three years or pay a fine of 2% of the land required for the construction of the saleable portion.

As of 2022, there were around 2,200 ongoing SRA projects in the city for which slum schemes had been submitted for and around 1,600 of them had also received Letter of Intent (LOI)

In these dead projects, around Rs 35,000 crore is stuck with the legitimate FIs. Developers who took money from FIs have failed to deliver the projects The amnesty scheme will help slum dwellers get homes and also help FIs recover heir money. This will also give a push to the housing market.

While the amnesty scheme was announced and gave the much needed push for slum projects across MMR, the implementation overall still looks sluggish and there are many slum schemes still in various stages of development

(Source: vlawpartners, economic times)

Chapter 16

Case Studies: North India

Unitech:

The new board of Unitech has earlier told the court currently, there are 74 (residential) and 10 (Commercial) under-construction projects wherein possession of about 15,000 units has to be delivered to homebuyers.

In its resolution plan, the new board of management has said that construction of 15,000 units has to be done for delivery of possession to homebuyers in three to four years, and at current price levels, the estimated cost of construction is Rs. 5,500-6,000 crores. It had said that if construction is not done, then the refund claims of these homebuyers will be approximately Rs 11,100 crores.

The forensic auditors had submitted their report, which said that Unitech Ltd received around Rs 14,270 crore from 29,800 home buyers from 2006-2014 and around Rs 1,805 crore from six financial institutions for the construction of 74 projects.

Current Status:

On April 26, 2024, the Supreme Court bench led by Chief Justice DY Chandrachud, alongside Justices JB Pardiwala and Manoj Misra, modified its earlier order asking Noida Authority to approve revised layouts of Unitech across all allocated land, regardless of outstanding dues exceeding Rs 10,000 crore.

After this prolonged legal battle, the supreme court order to start construction of Unitech stalled projects has come as a relief to around 6,000 homebuyers, but the funding concerns could ruin the joy.

In September 2024, Unitech Group resumed construction on its South Parks project in Gurugram Sector 70, after a more than 10-year-long delay. The project comprising 832 flats in 14 towers is expected to be completed within 36 months, the group said — the group was placed under new management appointed by the Supreme Court in 2020 after the previous management failed the complete the project

(Source: Economic Times)

Supertech:

Supertech Ltd has 38,041 customers, and out of them, homes have been delivered to 27,111 people. As many as 10,930 homes are yet to be delivered, and among them, over 70 per cent of construction is complete with respect to over 8,000 homes

Supertech Group said it would challenge the order before the National Company Law Appellate Tribunal (NCLAT). However, it also added the NCLT order will not affect the operations of other companies of the Supertech Group.

The NCLT order will not impact the construction at all ongoing projects or operation of the company, and "we are committed to giving delivery of units to allottees," it said.

The projects that will be impacted include Eco Village I, II and III in Greater Noida (West), known as Noida Extension, as well as the Emerald Court project, which houses the twin towers, according to a PTI report.

The debt of Supertech Ltd is around Rs 1,200 crore, including nearly Rs 150 crore loans from Union Bank of India.

The default pertains to the loan given by the Union Bank of India to the Eco Village II project at Greater Noida (West) in Uttar Pradesh, which was being developed at the cost of Rs 1,106.45 crore.

The Supreme Court ordered the demolition of Supertech's twin residential towers built in Noida after holding that the project was executed in violation of laws and involved an "unholy nexus" with the Noida Authority.

Figure 34: SuperTech Twin Towers Demolition

The order represents a big setback for the group led by RK Arora, which has increasingly found itself caught in disputes with property buyers over irregularities involving its projects.

Observing that there was collusion between Noida Authority and the builder in the construction of 40-storey twin towers in Noida, the Supreme Court on August 31 ordered the demolition of the structures located in Sector 93A within three months.

The court held that the construction violated the minimum distance requirement and had been built illegally without taking the consent of the individual flat owners as required under the UP Apartment Act.

The court said that the work of demolition should be carried out by Central Building Research Institute (CBRI) to ensure safe demolition. In case CBRI refuses, a new authority will be appointed, the bench said.

The Supertech Twin Towers were demolished on 28 August, 2022 after the decision by supreme court.

These towers were the highest structures in India to be demolished, the towers had a height of almost 100 metres — taller than the Qutub Minar. After much anticipation and a nine-year-long legal battle, the Supertech twin towers of Noida were reduced to rubble

(Source: NDTV, Indian Express)

Amrapali:

As many as 3,278 homebuyers of Amrapali Group are set to be declared as defaulters by a committee appointed by the Supreme Court to complete unfinished projects of the bankrupt real estate firm as they are still to enroll themselves on the dedicated portal for homebuyers and also make any payment towards their property purchases for the past few years.

A total of 32,000 homebuyers have enrolled so far on the portal created for the Amrapali home buyers, out of which about 7,000 have paid the full amount.

The exercise of tracking them and reaching out to them took three to four months, the total amount paid by the 3,278 homebuyers stood at around ₹200 crore- ₹300 crore.

The court receiver said that if any of these buyers, after being declared as defaulters, claim their investments, they would have to be refunded. He said also that the committee plans to have a contingency fund to meet such demands.

Meanwhile, another 7,000 people, who have registered on the platform, have not made any payment since 2019.

It also appointed state-run NBCC Ltd to complete 23 pending projects of Amrapali involving 46,000 stalled homes in Noida and Greater Noida, 41000+ already sold and around 5000+ unsold homes

NBCC has undertaken the completion of 650+ units in Noida and 4500 + units in 23 projects in Greater Noida under the aegis of Amrapali Stalled Projects and Investment Reconstruction Establishment (ASPIRE) and the supervision of the Supreme Court of India by 2022

Further, NBCC by October of 2023, has completed construction of around 13,500 homes of the stalled housing projects of Amrapali across Noida and Greater Noida and will be completing further 25,000 homes by approx. March, 2025

(Source: Livemint, Economic Times)

Chapter 17

Case Studies: Mumbai

Patra Chawl, Goregaon:

Siddharth Nagar Cooperative Housing Society also known as Patra Chawl, is a project first launched in 2007 but was stalled until it was inaugurated for development in Feb 2022

The Patra Chawl redevelopment case is a sordid saga of greed, corruption and betrayal that is being played out in hundreds of ageing housing societies across the city. These British-era barracks spread over 47 acres in Goregaon (W) house 672 residents who opted for redevelopment and moved out of their 265-sq-ft tenements in 2007, hoping to get homes twice the size in three years. Fourteen years later, their flats are yet to be built, and the builder has stopped paying them the rent. However, the sale component – three 24-storey towers are ready.

In the interim, 200 of the Patra Chawl tenement owners have expired. In 2007, the Maharashtra Housing and Area Development Authority (MHADA) gave the redevelopment contract of Patra Chawl to Guruashish Developers – a subsidiary of HDIL. Guruashish was also supposed to hand over 306 additional tenements to MHADA for distribution through its lottery system. It did neither. Instead, it sold land parcels and FSI from the project to eight other builders for Rs 1,034 crore.

Figure 35: Patra Chawl

It then went into insolvency in 2017. A 2018 report by the then housing secretary Sanjay Kumar found that an error in the calculation of the Patra Chawl area caused the state a loss of Rs 474 crore. Yet, it was only in March 2018 that MHADA filed an FIR against Guruashish

In February 2022, Chief Minister of Maharashtra virtually inaugurated the revived Patra Chawl redevelopment project.

Maharashtra Housing and Area Development Authority (MHADA) has been appointed as the nodal agency, and they have selected Relcon Infrastructure to execute this project.

The revival has given hope to 672 original tenants who will now each get 650 sq ft carpet flat.

Current Status:

While the project has all the approvals in place, construction has commenced on the plot but it is at a slow pace. While the rehabilitation commitment still remains to be fulfilled, the few sale towers which were not only ready but had people staying in it for years had faced issued relating to getting the occupation certificate, this was also resolved in 2023, as MHADA gave part OC to two of the projects

MHADA in April of 2023 issued OCs to A, C, D and B (partly) of Kalaptaru Radiance and A and B wing of Ekta Tripolis following the order of the Bombay High Court which provided relief to around 1,000 homebuyers

(Source: Free press Journal, money control)

Dharavi:

Announced in February 2004, the then chief minister Vilasrao Deshmukh announced the Dharavi revamp project, the state planned to convert large parts of the area — smack in the heart of the city and home to over one million people — into a world-class business centre with high-rise residential colonies.

The Dharavi revamp project was the brainchild of architect Mukesh Mehta, chairman MM Project Consultants Private Limited, who envisaged the plan in the late 1990s

The plan, to start with, was ambitious: 600 acres of Dharavi would be redeveloped. The slum was divided into five sectors and tenders would be issued simultaneously for all. The state formed the Dharavi Redevelopment Authority (DRA) and floated global tenders in 2007. The response was outstanding, too —101 companies took part in the process. However, over the years, the project languished and finally, in 2011, the process was cancelled.

This was partly due to the global slowdown, but as the tendering process dragged on, several of the selected bidders opted out citing a lack of clarity and delays in implementation. In 2009, a state-appointed experts' committee debunked the project.

Determination of eligibility was another issue that dogged the project: There are more than 200,000 hutments currently in Dharavi, but officially, only 69,160 are legal entities and eligible for new houses. In 2009, the Brihanmumbai Municipal Corporation (BMC) conducted a preliminary survey in Sector 4 and found that only 37% residents were eligible for new homes; the remaining 63 % weren't. This survey sparked fear that a majority of the people will be deprived of homes in this scheme.

In 2011, the state permitted MHADA, which had submitted a proposal the previous year, to redevelop Sector 5 of Dharavi. By 2016, 266 families moved into new homes. The same year, a new tender was floated for the other sectors, but the project failed to attract any bidders. However, fresh tenders were issued in 2018, and in February 2019, Seclink, a United Arab Emirates-based firm, was selected. The project was cancelled on the technical ground in October 2020.

One of the reasons why the project has also faced a problem from the residents are that only the residents have been considered for a long time for rehabilitation while others who have their livelihood in the area are ignored. The main issue was of eligibility, as residents said there are more than 200,000 hutments, whereas the official figure states that only 59,165 are legal entities eligible for new houses

Over the years, Dharavi has developed into a dynamic small scale manufacturing industry. Currently, it leads in garment manufacturing as well as food items. In addition, various items such as pottery, leather articles as well as recycling of plastics are carried out on a large scale. Most of the households undertake small scale work, which acts as support to this industry.

"What does this project hold for small entrepreneurs like us," said one of the residents who has a tailoring unit spread across 2,000 square feet on the first storey of his slum hutment. "I am not eligible for alternate place. In such circumstances, my ten workers and I will be on roads."

Figure 36: Dharavi

An informal survey in 2010, found that more than 80 % of the residents work in Dharavi itself; many industrial units have huge spaces inside slums where workers are housed; and entire families are often employed in small-scale manufacturing units in or around their homes, including in preparing food items.

Dharavi has a thriving informal economy, and this all will be destroyed if skyscrapers come up across Dharavi without taking cognisance of these issues. Once you formalise it, the price advantage will go away, and all things will become costlier. We need a welfare state concept where the government steps in without disrupting the existing economy of this place

Eighteen years on from 2004 to 2022, the project has moved at a snail's pace, and the dream of transforming over 600 acres of slum area remains a distant dream. Till date, only 350 residents have moved to new houses in the sector 5 area constructed by Maharashtra Housing and Area Development Authority (MHADA)

"The reason why Dharavi redevelopment is struck is due to lack of transfer of railway land. While about Rs 800 crore has been given to Railways, the land is yet to be transferred to us. I have also spoken to the Railways minister. These are some of the issues that need to be resolved," CM of Maharashtra, said in the Legislative assembly during the budget session in 2022

Current status:

New tender was rolled out in 2022 and the bid was won by Adani group's Adani Properties Private Limited to redevelop Dharavi. The work on Dharavi is currently ongoing, while there has been no construction activities on ground, there is a lot of buzz otherwise on the streets.

Dharavi is a unique blend of many people across different demographics living together. To capture the entire population along with the tenements, as per SRA, an Annexure II process is required which involves taking down details, measuring the unit sizes and coming out with final list of eligible tenements which will get a new house. Currently this process of the physical survey is ongoing in Dharavi among other activities running in parallel.

Given that some progress is also visible on ground and after talking to few stakeholders, this seems to be a project which can start soon with some on ground construction activity. Given the size and scale of the project, the SPV so created to fulfil the development obligation, will have to go full steam and start construction in full speed to adhere to the timeline

(Source: Hindustan Times, Liases Foras)

Kamathipura:

In the 1980s, MHADA carried out a comprehensive survey as the first step toward transforming the entire neighbourhood through an urban renewal proposal, but this project was stalled, citing financial risks. In 2005, a local private developer expressed his interest in undertaking redevelopment of a large part of Kamathipura.

However, these grand plans were stalled when the real estate market crashed in 2008. In 2016, the Kamathipura Landlords Welfare Association was formed, which brought together almost 400 landlords. Their plan was to convert Kamathipura into a township of 24 towers, parks and gardens, wider roads and public amenities. This too, fell through due to lack of consensus between landlords and tenants, especially with respect to the size of apartments and compensations.

Figure 37: Kamathipura

In March 2020, the Maharashtra government approved a large scale cluster redevelopment project for Kamathipura although that too has now been stalled due to the ongoing COVID pandemic.

An individual aged around 60 years and a resident of Kamathipura, shudders every time there are heavy showers. The reason: his 100-year-old building, which is supported by scaffolding, is in a dilapidated condition, and local authorities have warned that it can collapse at anytime. "Our buildings which are more than a century old, have outlived their utility and are not repairable. They can collapse anytime," said the resident

He lives in Kamathipura, the infamous red-light area in south Mumbai, and the majority of these structures are more than 100 years old.

As per the various report, Kamathipura has 16 lanes with 500 buildings in which there are 3858 rooms and 778 shops. A total area of 39.8 Acres will be redeveloped, having 800 Landlords and 8000+ tenants.

The project is ambitious and will be developed under the cluster redevelopment scheme. Each tenant will be offered approx. 508 sq ft carpet flat against their current treatment, while each landlord will also be offered a approx. 500 sq ft of carpet flat for every 50 sqmt plot area. Additionally, those holding tenements on plots the size of 51- to 100-square meters will be eligible for two flats measuring 500-square feet each; and for every 151- to 200-square meter plot the owner would be eligible for four flats measuring 500-square feet each and so on

Housing Minister of Maharashtra said, "People have been staying in this area since 1961. Around 8000 families will get a new house. Existing landlords and tenants, broths will get new homes. We have 100% consent from the residents and the work will start soon."

Figure 38: Kamathipura

The project named 'Urban Village: Kamathipura township', focusing on the redevelopment of Kamathipura, will be initiated in three months, the Housing Minister said in March 2022 that there are about 8500 houses, and each will get a 500 square feet house.

Current status:

All the permissions are in place and the redevelopment project was expected to soon take off, once it was given a green light but there exist no on ground progress. All the structures still stand today, construction activity is yet to start.

MHADA, which is the nodal agency of the project, had appointed a consultant to prepare a detailed project report (DPR) and request for proposal (RFP). "The DPR and RFP are ready and we are soon going to float tenders for the project," the official from the housing department said.

BDD Chawl:

Bombay Development Directorate chawls, also famously known as BDD Chawls. The British had constructed the 207 BDD chawls around 1920 as low-cost housing for mill workers, dock workers, civic and other government employees.

The BDD chawls are spread over 93 acres and comprise 207 ground-plus-three-storey buildings, having 16,557 flats measuring 160 sq ft.

Out of these BDD chawls are present in three areas namely Worli, NM Joshi Marg and Naigaon

The Worli BDD Chawl redevelopment project contract was awarded in January 2019, while contracts for the Naigoan and NM Joshi Marg BDD Chawl projects were awarded in March 2017

Currently, the construction work for new buildings has begun albiet at a slow pace than anticipated.

Figure 39: BDD Chawls

Tata Projects Limited, Capacit'e Infraprojects Ltd and Citic Group Consortium, secured the Rs 11,744-crore order for the BDD Chawl redevelopment at Worli, Mumbai.

As part of the BDD Chawl redevelopment, tenants currently staying in 160 sq ft houses will get the 500 sq ft house which is three times the existing BDD Chawl unit's size

The entire project will be around Rs 17,000 crore project — involving 121 buildings in Worli, 42 at Naigaon, and 32 at NM Joshi Marg in Lower Parel—will come up in multiple phases, according to officials in charge of the project.

The project will not only house existing tenants but also create an additional stock of 10,000 housing units

Plans to redevelop the rundown chawls have been in the pipeline for more than two decades, but little progress was made because no private builders came forward to take up the project and residents, too, were resistant.

MHADA has appointed private contractors for each area — L&T Realty for Naigaon, Shapoorji Pallonji for NM Joshi Marg, and Tata Projects for Worli. The redevelopment model has been designed such that contractors can raise bills on the basis of costs they incur for the period of the contract. This makes MHADA own the entire risk of any project delays or litigation against the project, and has emboldened bidders to come forward and implement the gargantuan project.

Current Status:

The project has been started at various locations with some chawls being demolished and tenants shifted out of the current accommodation. *(Source: ThePrint)*

Several issues of residents' remain unresolved, one such instance is that of Some residents have not yet received their agreements, and many are struggling to receive the promised monthly rent from the Maharashtra Housing and Area Development Authority (MHADA). Earlier they were promised 11 months' rent in advance but are actually getting only 1 month rent as a time. Each tenement that did not opt for transit camp be it residential or non-residential is eligible for Rs 25,000 monthly rent. The MHADA in June 2024 agreed to give the tenements 11 months' rent in advance.

While the work is currently on at most of the sites mentioned above, the progress is much slower than anticipated, while earlier estimates as of last year too for completion of the project was 2026; in our opinion, seeing the construction timelines, phasing, on ground realities, delays be it procedural or due to other reason, it is most likely that the completion will be pushed by a few months if not more

Motilal Nagar:

Spread across 142 acres in Goregaon is a prime land, the winning bidder has to rehabilitate 5,300 families which include the construction of 3,700 MHADA houses and 1,600 hutments. The residents will be given 1,600 sq ft houses. Besides, the winner also has to construct a mini township with schools, dispensaries and open spaces.

Maharashtra Housing and Area Development Authority (MHADA) would be the nodal agency overseeing this ₹30,000 crore project.

Motilal Nagar was built in 1960 to house people belonging to the economically weak sections. Though it has 200 sq ft houses, many have illegally extended their rooms. In the last few years, several builders have been offering redevelopment proposals to the residents. Currently top two bidders have offered 1600 sq ft houses, 8 times their current tenantments but the residents want 2,000 sq ft houses, i.e. ten times their current houses.

Figure 40: Motilal Nagar

Even this present tender has come under scanner as some top builders accused MHADA of deliberately adding the ₹9000 crore net worth clause to exclude them from the bidding process.

According to an official, the MHADA has decided to undertake an integrated redevelopment of the colonies which envisages rehabilitation of buildings for both existing eligible residential and commercial users, markets, shopping centres, offices, houses and work-places, mixed-use buildings, cultural centres, public halls, recreational centres, schools, healthcare centres and residential buildings of various sizes of apartments for sale.

After redevelopment, nearly 33,000 flats will be available.

Current Status:

The Maharashtra state housing department and MHADA has given its nod to the project and are expected to start construction on the site soon. The project has yet not kicked-off despite it being cleared in 2021. There are some litigations ongoing in the court of law for this project.

Additionally, the Motilal Nagar Vikas Samiti, an association of residents wrote a letter to PMO alleging a mega Scam as tender cost for the project envisaged in the tender increased by 60% in just 6 months from Rs 21,918 crores to Rs 36,295 crores and MHADA share going down to 13% from earlier 20%.

The association also highlighted the fact that the cost for 142 acre Motilal Nagar at given above is much higher than the redevelopment of Dharavi which is 600 acres and costs envisaged is around Rs 22,000 crore.

With all this, the project is yet to see the light of day by actual construction yet to start, currently there seems to be little progress when it comes to actual construction activities at ground level at Motilal Nagar

Azad Nagar:

The proposed redevelopment project was earlier supposed to be developed by East & West developers, a part of RNA Group. However, tenants were upset as the firm stopped the payment of rents since 2017. Following which after much opposition, in 2020, the redevelopment agreement with East & West developer was terminated by the Brihanmumbai Municipal Corporation (BMC)

In 2006, BMC, the developer and the residents of Azad Nagar Chawl had signed a tripartite agreement. The project was to be developed under development Control Regulation DCR 33(7). In 2015, all 32 chawls of the ground structure comprising 320 tenants was demolished. From 2017, East & West developers stopped paying them rents.

Figure 41: Azad Nagar

Figure 42: illustration of Redeveloped Towers

After a delay of over 18 years, tenants of Azad Nagar CHS of Wadala will finally see their houses being redeveloped as early as next year. Godrej Properties Ltd, a leading developer, has entered into an agreement to redevelop the said housing project spread across 7.5 acres of land parcel in 2021

Current Status:

Project was revived successfully and is underway, construction has started after the intervention and is being developed by a Godrej Properties Limited. (Source: Free Press Journal)

The Project is named as Godrej Horizon, existing tenements have been shifted out on rent basis and the construction of project is on in full swing and on track for successful delivery not only to erstwhile flat owners but also to the new ones who have bought the flat in the sale towers.

Others:

- Chikalwadi Chawl located in Tardeo, redevelopment was stuck since 2007 as few tenants did not vacate the premises has finally resumed after 15 years with the private developer being roped in. MHADA had approved for Cluster Redevelopment Scheme, wherein all the erstwhile tenants would get 583 sq ft of usable carpet area along with a Rs 6 lakh corpus fund. The Plot spread across 1.54 acres plot housing a chawl will make way for a 36 storey tower to be jointly developed by Shreepati Skies and Man Infraconstruction.

  (Source: Construction World, projectstoday)

- Safalya CHS located in Tilak Nagar, had its redevelopment stuck since 2007 has also finally resumed and chosen to self-redevelop after being harassed by the developer for over 15 years. Its construction is ongoing and National Cooperative Union of India (NCUI) impressed with successful resolution of the case has highlighted this one as a role model to encourage self-development and will be introduced in the training modules for the entire nation

Section E

Self-Redevelopment

Chapter 1

Concept of Self Redevelopment

Self-development is one in which the construction process is carried out by members of society who have the conveyance in their names. In this, individuals or groups of individuals come together and redevelop the said property together instead of approaching the builder.

In today's rapidly changing world, the demand for housing is growing simultaneously. In cities like Mumbai or other cities, which have become huge Metropolitan areas in the last few decades and have a huge population residing and working in the city, this demand has literally exploded exponentially. In Mumbai, where land availability is very short, and the need for housing is still growing rapidly, redevelopment is the only feasible option.

Many of the buildings/societies in Mumbai have passed their useful life and became a risk for the resident to live in the old building as they have become dilapidated or structurally weak. To avoid danger and to replace the old building with new, redevelopment is the only feasible and fast-paced solution which has benefits for all the stakeholders involved.

In the case of Self-redevelopment, society itself takes the developer's work by appointing the best Architect/ Project Management Consultants. They take the responsibility of providing the best quality homes and amenities to society members. The Maharashtra Government has taken the initiative to launch Self-Redevelopment Scheme in January 2018. This step by the Government encourages Cooperative Housing Societies to undertake redevelopment of their building and boost self-redevelopment Projects in Mumbai. Self-Redevelopment has become a better and safer alternative to redevelopment in Mumbai.

Real estate developers are also witnessing one of the most difficult recessions in decades. The real estate industry cycle in India has been going through a lower trajectory and has been facing recession since about 2013, when the prices have remained relatively stagnant. The triple whammy of regulations posed further huge challenges to the industry:

1. Real Estate (Regulation and Development) Act, 2016

2. Demonetization in November of 2016

3. Goods and Services Tax implemented from 2017

All of this has led to price stagnation, lower growth, delayed recovery in the industry, and reduced developer margins. It has also led to a consolidation in the industry where big builders with a good brand presence have gained market share, and many small-time developers have seen themselves out of business. Given the industry's overall scenario and the fear of being stuck in the middle, there will be no time for negotiating with the developer. This has opened a new door for society to take advantage of the opportunity for property redevelopment, titled "Self-Redevelopment."

Chapter 2

Comparative Analysis

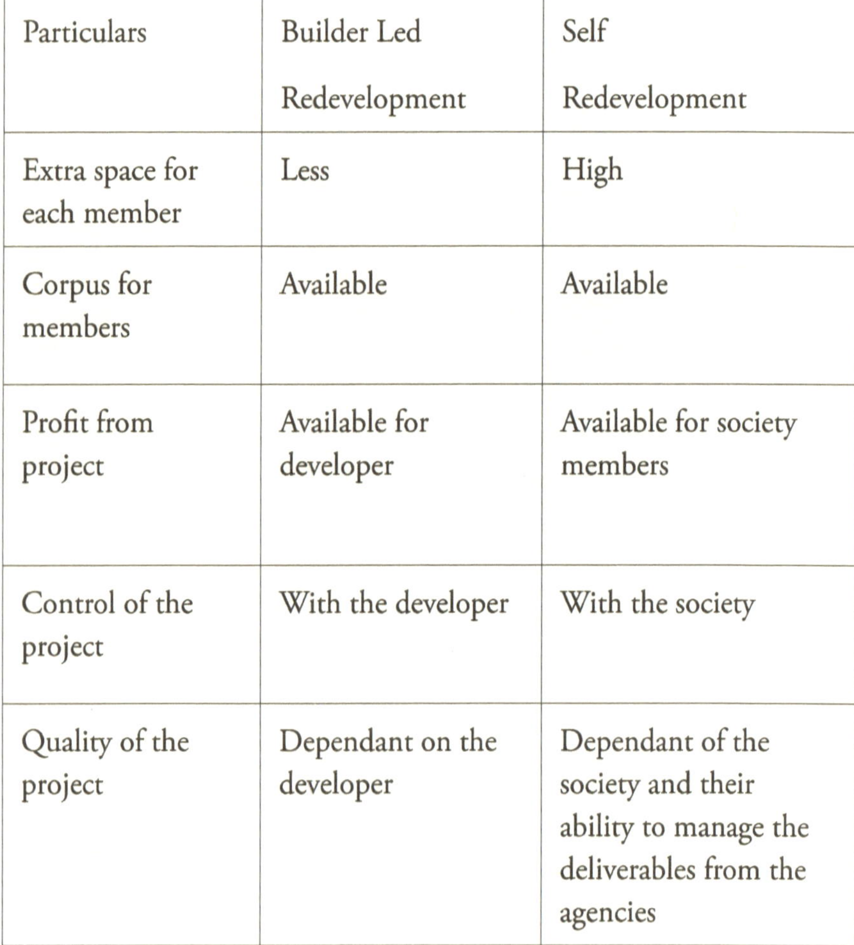

Particulars	Builder Led Redevelopment	Self Redevelopment
Extra space for each member	Less	High
Corpus for members	Available	Available
Profit from project	Available for developer	Available for society members
Control of the project	With the developer	With the society
Quality of the project	Dependant on the developer	Dependant of the society and their ability to manage the deliverables from the agencies

Designs and Plans	In the name of the developer	In the name of the society
Design as per members needs	Has the authority to change designs without society consent	Designs made as per member's needs
Fund Management	Developers Control Confidential	Society's control Transparent
Funds allotted for rent	PDCs for only 6 to 12 months or monthly cheques	Society's Control
Expertise for the entire project	Has the experience in-house and or works with his networks	Empanels different experts/ agencies required across the project timeline through known networks or tendering
Timely completion of project	Can be delayed	Society's ability to manage different resources and the entire program

Funds for the project	Developer put his own money/ gets investments	Society generates money through self-funding or loans from financial institutions
Dealing with Municipal and other authorities	Has experience in dealing with the authorities	Dependant on outsourced agency or do it by self
Knowledge about the entire process	Has the requisite know-how	Doesn't have all the requisite knowledge
Managing the entire program and all the experts/ agencies	Has the requisite management capability	Maybe available in the society or dependant on external experts/ agencies
Risk Management	In favour of developer	Society's ability to see the different risks, prioritize them and take timely appropriate decisions

(Source: WeRedevelopment, 2022)

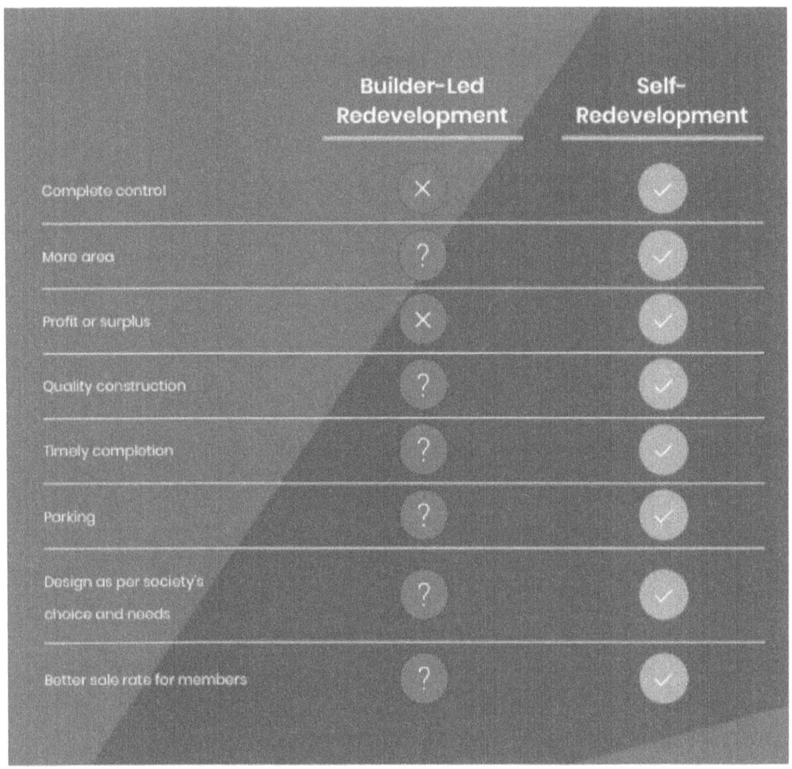

Developers Prospect with Fixed Overheads

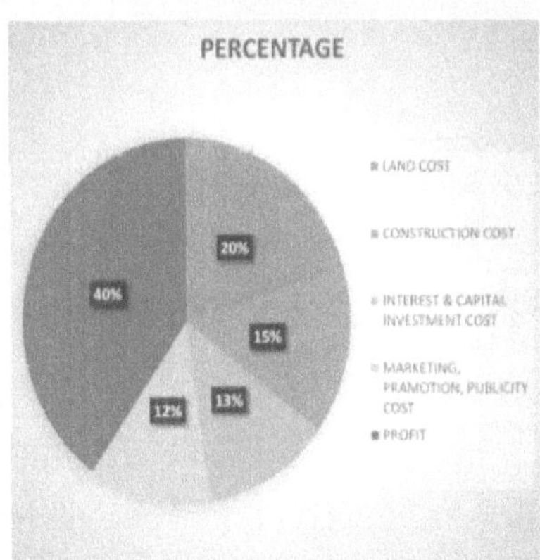

Self – Redevelopment Prospect with Executor

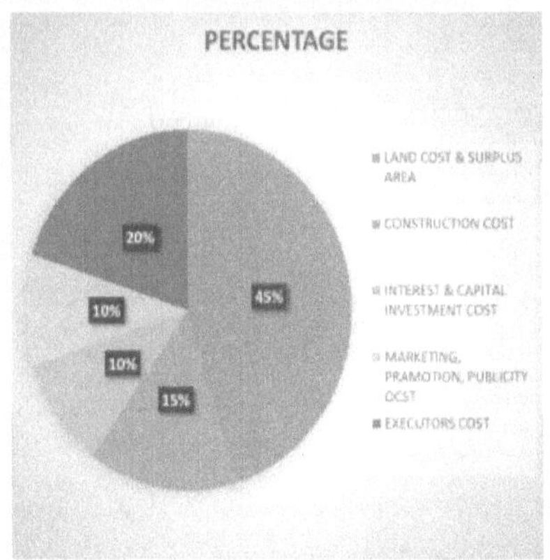

Chapter 3

Need for Self-Redevelopment

As explained in the earlier part of this section, Self-Redevelopment has been seeing an increasing trend and keen interest from many stakeholders. The need for it is profound and clearly understood by the points given below:

- Many stalled projects across the region:

  Mumbai has seen one of the most stalled projects across the region, they have been stalled due to many reasons.

  As such Self Redevelopment has come up as a possible solution which can be one of the fastest ways to develop many buildings in Mumbai

- Trust in the builder community:

  The trust on the community has reduced over the years because of cases involving fraud and cheating. Quite a few individual cases have tainted the entire community, due to which the trust on the builder has eroded over the years.

  Due to this trust erosion, there is a dire need for Self-Development, as the builder is by passed and the society members directly develop the project

- Long timelines for the completion of the projects:

  Due to many permissions, stakeholders and other requirements the timeline for a redevelopment project are very long. The builder usually extends the timeline due to cash flow issues, other reasons of their own.

  In this case Self Development can be a plausible solution as the project will adhere to Strict timelines and deliverables

- Unpaid dues to the old tenants:

  In many of the projects it has been seen in the past that there have been dues which have been unpaid to tenants. One of the major issues for tenants is payment of rent by the developer which in quite a few cases go unpaid.

  In case of Self Development this issue will be sorted as the tenants themselves develop the property

Chapter 4

Advantages of Self-Redevelopment

In this chapter we will try and understand the advantages that Self-Redevelopment has to offer

- Benefits to society members:
    - Society members benefit by receiving additional Carpet Area, Corpus Fund and Rent in case of Self-Redevelopment
    - They also retain the profits that would be traditionally earned by the developer, which are distributed among the society members in any of the above ways as stated, i.e. additional carpet area, corpus fund and rent.
    - They have the freedom to decide on the Amenities, Specifications, Brands & Makes of fixtures they would want in their new building.
- Interest Rates:

    Banks offer a much cheaper interest rate to the societies that have decided for self- redevelopment as compared to the interest rate provided to the developer in the actual market. According to the latest updates, such societies will be charged a 4% interest subsidy on construction loans.

- Other Charges:

  Due to Self-Redevelopment, the society eventually has savings in Stamp Duty, Registration Charges, other premiums payable to the municipal authorities, and Development Agreement with the Developer. Such societies will also be charged a lower premium for the paid FSI component, which go in for Self-Redevelopment

- Better Transparency:

  As the society has the freedom and flexibility to appoint the Consultants and Contractors, the overall control of the redevelopment project is with society members. This results in better decision making and no hidden knowledge or information on anyone's part

- Timely Completion:

  Speedy and timely completion of the project is one of the main advantages of self-redevelopment as the society members are directly involved in the process, apart from the PMC appointed. Also, the completion is a given due to assured fund supply from the bank, society members and other financial intermediaries, if any

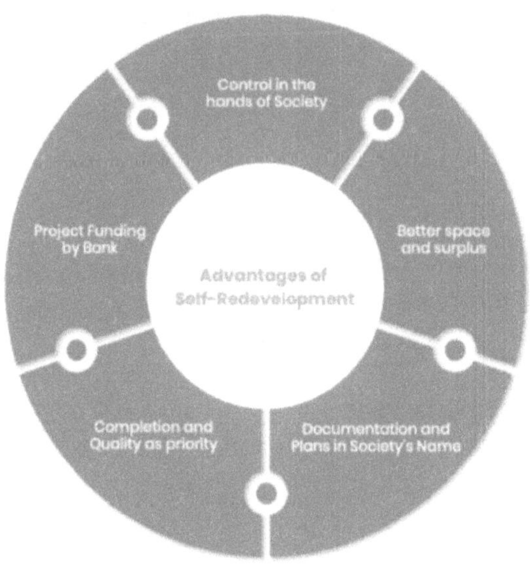

Chapter 5

Stakeholder Analysis

Any kind of development or construction of a building involves many stakeholders coming together to finish the project, it involves constant coordination and timely implementation by all involved to help the project see the light of the day.

Self-Redevelopment model is no different, although here the developer is replaced by the society, there are still many stakeholders involved, they are as given below:

- Society Members
- Consultants: Architects, Lawyers, Chartered Accountants
  - Accountants
  - Advocates
  - Architects
  - BMS specialists
  - Brokering Agency
  - Civil Contractor
  - Concrete Specialists
  - Designers
  - Electricians
  - Elevation Experts

- Fabricators
- Fire and Security Engineers
- Fire Safety Experts
- Geotechnical `Engineers
- Ground workers
- HVAC Experts
- Interior Designers
- Investors/Financial Institutes
- Landscape Gardeners
- Liaisoning Architect
- Lift Consultants
- Main Contractor/Builders
- MEPF Consultant
- Painting Contractor
- Parking Consultants
- Pest Control
- Planning Consultants
- Plumbers
- Project Managers
- Quantity Surveyors
- RCC Consultants
- RMC
- Sales /Marketing Consultants
- Services Engineers
- Signage Consultant
- Site Supervisor

- Structural Engineers

- Surveyors

- Water Proofing specialist

Figure 17: Construction Workers

Figure 18: Civil Engineers

Figure 19: Surveyors, Supervisors

Figure 20: Project Manager

Figure 21: Institute of Chartered Accountants of India

Figure 22: Bar Council of India

- Project management company

- Development Manager (Contractor)

- Financial Institution and Investors

- Government and other approving authorities:

- Development Planning Dept
- Town Planning Dept
- Assessment Dept
- Hydraulic Dept
- Sewerage Dept
- Traffic Dept
- Storm Water Drainage Dept
- Collector's Office
- Tree Authority
- Airport Authority of India
- Pest Control Authority
- MTNL
- Fire Department
- PDW
- Water Dept
- Tehsildar Office
- BMC
- MHADA
- Customers

Figure 23: BMC

Figure 24: BMC Headquarters

Figure 25: MHADA

Figure 26: AAI

As per GR, MHADA (Maharashtra Housing and Area Development Authority) and MDDC Bank (Mumbai District Central Cooperative Bank) and PMC play a vital role in Self Redevelopment Scheme.

MHADA- Helps to get all required permission quickly for self-redevelopment.

MDDC Bank- This Bank is authorised to provide loan to self-redevelopment projects.

<u>PMC</u> – A Project Management Consultant helps and guides the housing society in the overall process of self-redevelopment. PMC helps in planning, executing, monitoring, decision making, ensuring quality standards and following government rules and norms. It provides various professionals involved in the self-redevelopment process and fulfils the requirements of society and its members.

Chapter 6

Process of Self-redevelopment

The checklist for initiating a self-development project begins with obtaining a conveyance in society's name, implying that society should be the Landowner.

The various steps involved in the process of Self Redevelopment are explained in this chapter. In Self Re-Development, there are several activities to be carried out. Some activities start from the date members request for Redevelopment until the members are rehoused in the redeveled building with a completion certificate. These activities are called continuous activities. The methods or the steps to be taken for Self-Re-Development are as under:

STEP 1: DECIDE BETWEEN REDEVELOPMENT OR SELF REDEVELOPMENT:

20% or more percentage of the society's total members need to request the Managing Committee to convene the Special General Body meeting to decide about Redevelopment or Self Redevelopment as outlined in the Government order dated July 4 2019.

The detailed procedure to convene the Special General Body meeting with 14 days clear notice, its quorum to be 2/3rd of total members and the decision to be taken by more than 51% of the total members etc. The minutes and documents to be maintained by the society are explained in detail in the Government order for Redevelopment dated July 4 2019, issued under section 79A of the MCS Act, 1960.

STEP 2: APPOINTMENT OF PROJECT MANAGEMENT CONSULTANTS AND ADVOCATE OR LEGAL CONSULTANTS:

Once the society with more than 51% of total members decides to proceed with Redevelopment through the builder or by the society themselves under Self Re-Development, the society needs to appoint a project management consultant. The entire process laid down in the notification dated July 4 2019, may be followed. There is no need to give any advertisement to appoint the professionals or project management consultants, or the advocate. The managing committee or the members may refer good professionals with their consent and quote for their services.

Without PMC and the Advocate appointment, society should not take any further steps in the Redevelopment. These professionals shall guide the members of the society to take up the best redevelopment methods with advantages and challenges.

STEP 3: FEASIBILITY REPORT:

Once the society decides to proceed with the Redevelopment and the necessary PMC is appointed, the Architect may be asked to provide a feasibility report under different Development Control Regulations and recommend the one best suitable to society.

The feasibility report also needs to consider the various incentives provided under Government Order for Self-Redevelopment dated September 13 2019 (date to be confirmed). The feasibility report should cover various options for re-development, such as –

- Redevelopment through the developer

- Self-Re-Development under the regular scheme of Redevelopment

- Self-Re-Development under PMAY with 2.5 FSI by giving 35% of the saleable area to Govt for allotting to eligible PMAY beneficiaries.

The feasibility report under different systems of Self-Redevelopment like Departmental system, Package Deal system, Barter System or Development Management System also may be prepared and circulated to the members for their better understanding. The challenges involved in implementing each of the systems of Self Re-Development and how such challenges can be mitigated by the members' active participation and involving the professionals and the financial institution need to be explained.

As per the document available with society, a feasibility report should be prepared, considering the following points:

- To ascertain the maximum permissible carpet area available in the project based on various applicable regulations, such as DCPR-2034 for Mumbai.

- To calculate the total project cost, which includes the construction cost, approval cost (including the purchase of TDR), Fungible Area premium FSI, and all other premiums, fees, deposits, rent for existing tenements during the construction period, Corpus Fund to Society or its members, and miscellaneous costs. Interest on blocked capital, and so on.

- Determine the minimum carpet area needed to be sold to recover the entire project cost.

- After providing the above, the remaining carpet area can be distributed/shared amongst the existing members.

- Evaluation of the preceding steps to finalise the proposal strategy.

STEP 4: RAISING OF FUNDS FOR THE PROJECT – THE WAYS, MEANS AND SOURCES OF FINANCING:

The main challenge in self-development is raising funds needed for project implementation from start to finish, i.e. from the beginning of the project until the completion certificate and occupation certificate are received. There are different sources and methods to raise the required funds. Society needs to work out at least three or four alternative plans to raise funds by involving the experts.

Following are some of the ways or sources to raise funds. Society needs to evaluate each of the sources or methods and then take the appropriate decision.

- Purchasing a part of the available sale area by existing society members to raise initial finance for the project.

- Purchasing the remaining sale area by Society members' relatives, friends and people from their close circle.

- Advertisement for balance sale area or appointing an agency, to sale this area.

- Appointing sole-selling agents to sell the available balance sell area

- Borrowing loans from reputed banks / financial institutions.

- After a detailed discussion with the Society members, the best available finance options need to be finalised. In short, taking the lead and action on finance arrangements.

STEP 5: BOOKING OF ADDITIONAL AREA REQUIRED FOR THE MEMBERS AT THE PRICE FIXED BY THE SOCIETY BASED ON THE FEASIBILITY REPORT:

Once the society freezes Self Re-Development and the prices at which the area is to be sold to the members, society should invite the members to apply for the additional area's requirement by paying the amount as per the cost price or with a nominal increase. These exercises will also help society decide the balance area to be sold in the market and the accessible funds available from the members.

STEP 6: ARCHITECTURAL PLANNING/DESIGNING:

Once the society decides to proceed in Self-Redevelopment based on the feasibility report and the funding arrangement approved by the society, the next step would be to prepare the plans for the existing members with free of cost additional area to be allotted to the members on additional area purchased by the members.

Experts required:

- Design Architect
- Structural Engineer

As per the strategy finalised in the Feasibility Report, prepare a plan for the redevelopment proposal; the Architect and his team will consider the existing members' requirements and consider the sale area aspect. Further, they will take cognisance of various Development Control Regulations and existing site conditions.

The Architect will also take the help of a Structural Engineer to prepare necessary structural drawings and if any alternatives need to be done in the proposed plan.

After finalising the draft plan and taking stakeholders' responses thereon, the team will prepare final plans, a schematic view of the building etc. (here, the etc. would be a 3-D walkthrough and building model).

The plans need to be circulated to the members and obtain their written consent on the plans so that the members should not object on any account in due course.

STEP 7: PREPARATION OF REDEVELOPMENT PROPOSAL FOR ITS SUBMISSION TO THE BUILDING PROPOSAL DEPARTMENT OF BMC:

Experts required:

- Design Architect and the Liaison Architect
- Civil Engineer registered with BMC as licensed Surveyor
- Liaoning Team, as assistants.

As per the plans finalised by the Design Architect, the Liaison Architect will prepare Municipal Drawings, and his Liaison team will also obtain various documents required to be submitted, along with the proposal, to Building Proposal Department.

PMC and his team will guide society to obtain various NOCs, such as CFO NOC and EETC NOC, etc.

Liaison Architect will process the file to obtain approval for the proposal's concessions from the Hon'ble Municipal Commissioner, proposing to consume the entire FSI, including Premium FSI and TDR Fungible. However, once the Municipal Commissioner approves the concessions required for the entire proposal, the IOD may be obtained in parts to minimise initial investment.

Obtain IOD and CC.

Guide Society to obtain TDR from the open market and process the field for TDR deduction from its DRC. However, as per the Government Circular dated September 13, 2019, societies opting for such TDR from the Planning Authority itself should be able to avail of the same at the rate of 50% of the Ready Reckoner Rate as proposed in GR for Self Redevelopment. This will benefit society in terms of cost-saving and the hassle of buying TDR from the open market and processing for deduction of the same.

STEP 9: STRUCTURAL DESIGNING:

Experts required:

- Structural Designer, i.e. Civil Engineer.

As per the final plans, Structural Engineers will prepare Structural Drawings for the proposed building in the most cost-effective manner while fulfilling all requisite conditions.

STEP 9: SELECTION OF A CONTRACTOR, THROUGH TENDERING PROCESS, WHO THEN WOULD BE CARRYING OUT THE ENTIRE WORK DEPATMENTALLY OF BY OUTSOURCING IT FOR VARIOUS WORKS AND THE SAME SHALL INCLUDE THE FOLLOWING POINTS:

The society architect, Engineer and other professionals involved will prepare a detailed tender for each contractor and service provider. Some of the critical aspects that have to be covered in the tender documents are as follows:

- Specification of work

- Specification of material brands and their quality

- Resources/infrastructure available with the contractor

- Financial capability of the contractor

- To verify at the site, as per the list provided by the contractor, of his completed projects

- Conditions of a contract offer from bidders

- Legal points of tender documents, penalty clauses & termination causes.

- Minimum possible cost of the project

STEP 10: LEGAL WORKS OF TENDER DOCUMENTS WILL INCLUDE:

Experts required:

- Legal Advisor

- Civil Contractor

- Project manager

The tender document should include the following:-

- Completion period

- Payment release dates

- Reporting system

- Discipline on site

- The infrastructure required on site

- Supervision and monitoring systems

- Penalty clauses

- Termination points

STEP 11: PROJECT PLANNING: BAR CHART, CPM / PERT – THE TIME SCHEDULE OF THE PROJECT WILL INCLUDE THE FOLLOWING MAIN POINTS:

Experts required

- • Project Manager
- • Civil Engineers

Project planning should include the following

- Each activity of the project to be carried out
- Time required for each activity
- Cash flow requirement for each activity
- Penalty clauses & termination clauses
- Quality checkpoints of each activity
- Reporting/monitoring system
- Weekly / monthly feedback meetings schedule
- Feedback reports to the society

STEP 12: EXECUTION OF PROJECT:

Experts required:

- • Project manager
- • Project coordinator
- • Design Architect
- • Civil Engineer
- • Charted Accountant
- • Quality Controller

- • Site Supervisor

The following points need to be adhered to while considering the execution of the project:

- Monitoring the project as per the approved plans and the schedule finalised

- Supervising each of the activities every day

- Controlling things, not happening as per planning and its schedule

- Checking the quality of every material delivered on site

- Co-ordination meetings with all team members

- Feedback meetings at regular intervals with the society members

STEP 13: POST-CONSTRUCTION STAGE:

Experts required:

- • Project manager

- • Design Architect

- • Civil Engineer

Post Construction stage involves the following:-

- Closing the project by all means

- Settling bills of all vendors, contractors and consultants

- Settling of the load account

- To prepare and provide a file of 'As Built Drawings' to the society

- To preserve in a separate file all documents of guarantees/warranties.

- To hand over all the agreements executed and other documents carried out with the contractors and various agencies.

- To provide RERA carpet area certificates to facilitate the processing of Occupation Certificate from BMC

- To acquire Occupation Certificate for the project
- To obtain from the BMC, the Building Completion Certificate of a redevelopment project.

CONTINUOUS ACTIVITIES TO BE DONE UNDER EACH OF THE ABOVE STEPS:

As explained at the beginning of this chapter, there are some essential activities of administration, monitoring, supervision, sale etc., which may be considered continuous activities to be done at each of the steps explained above. They are briefly explained as under:

Administration:

Experts required

- • Administrative manager
- • Civil Engineer
- • Office staff

1. PMC Team provides Legal, Architectural, Engineering and works coordination services under one roof.

2. PMC will keep one Administration person stationed at your society as a one-point contact for all the project's above work.

3. All the documentation, paying of the rent amounts, of tenants/ occupants and demolition procedures of the structures existing at the site

4. All the activities of these redevelopments will be informed to society well in advance

5. RERA Registration and related compliance work.

6. All the legal, Architectural, Engineering work will be executed, monitored by PMC's expert's administration team.

7. PMC have a periodic reporting system in place (To society) for all the projects

8. All the records will be retained and handed over to the society at the end of each activity. PMC to have a complaint/inquiry slot kept in every periodic progress meeting, which is conducted in all the stakeholders of the project

MARKETING OF THE SALEABLE FLATS TO GENERATE REQUIRED FUNDS FOR REDEVELOPMENT:

Experts required

*   Project manager

*   Business development manager

*   Chartered accountant

1. Marketing saleable areas to society's own original members.

2. Marketing saleable area to original member's relatives, friends and people from their close circle.

3. Advertisement for the saleable area, by hoardings and in newspapers

4. Appointing a professional agency to sale this area under PMC's monitoring

5. Monitoring and guiding selling agency for the rate expected, available area, request to adopt fast-selling techniques, a minimum final sale rate, etc.

6. Attending to on-site enquires from prospective customers.

7. Facilitating closing of the sale

8. Maintaining payment schedules

Chapter 7

Government Resolution on Self- Redevelopment

Mumbai has been a port city, surrounded by water and has scarce land, but the demand for housing is growing continuously. Some of the buildings in Mumbai and other cities are old, their structural strength is depleting, and it's not safe for the tenant. Over 14,000 building in Mumbai alone is not safe. Redevelopment through developers is a bit tricky as we see developers' track record in the past decade. The Government had to step in to protect the interest of the tenant.

(TOI, 2019)

To ease the tenant's hardship, a government resolution (GR) dated September 13 2019, was issued by the Government of Maharashtra. As per the resolution, the Maharashtra Housing and Area Development Authority (MHADA) is the scheme's supervising authority. Under this scheme, the MHADA must give one window system for all the mandatory permissions required for the CHS's self-redevelopment. This can make sure that the requisite permissions are given quicker than it might otherwise take. MHADA must list a project management consultant (PMC), architects and construction contractors to provide choices to the housing CHS and to pick the right professional needed for self-redevelopment. The Mumbai District Central Cooperative Bank (the Bank) will provide the CHS loan for self-redevelopment.

Eligibility criteria for Self-Redevelopment:

Cooperative housing societies of Maharashtra which are registered are eligible for the self-redevelopment; any other resident's welfare association will not be eligible to avail of the advantages of the self-redevelopment scheme. Only buildings which are 30-year-old or more would be eligible for the advantages. This period of 30 years will be counted from the date of receipt of the Occupation Certificate or the date of the first assessment of the land tax by the local authority.

Single-Window system for all approvals:

Various approvals are required to redevelop any property from various departments and government authorities; they are time-consuming and interlinked. The Government has realised that the CHS undertaking self-redevelopment is not doing business but developing their own house. To avoid delay and save Costs for redevelopment, GR introduced a single-window system for making applications and granting approvals.

The time limit for approvals:

Usually, the planning authority takes they're on time for approvals; any delay in approvals will affect the redevelopment process. So, the Government initiated that approvals should be granted in six months from the date of application for self-redevelopment. Any objection by the authority also needed to be pointed out between 7 to 15 days. Most of the work is handled by having online submissions and approvals of the plan.

Period for completion of a self-redevelopment project:

Housing societies that opt for a self-redevelopment scheme have to complete the project within three years. If there is a phase-wise development, phase-wise approvals can be taken. Once the approvals are taken for a phase, it should be completed in 3 years. The three years is considered from the day the society building is demolished.

Benefit of extra FSI:

- The Government has considered three different situations for FSI incentive.

- Housing Societies opting for a self-redevelopment scheme will get 10% extra FSI, over and above what is entitled to the area's redevelopment regulation. This will encourage societies to undertake self-redevelopment.

- If the rehab area for the resident is more than the permissible FSI, 10% more FSI would be given

- If the road width is less than 9 meters; the building should be given 0.4 FSI without premium instead of the present 0.25 FSI.

Transferable development rights:

TDR is generally to be purchased from the market. To ease the hardship, the Government has given CHS benefits opting for self-redevelopment. It will get a concessional rate of 50% of the ready reckoner rate from the concerned planning authority. CHS can opt for complete approvals with the loading of TDR, FSI, etc., from the authority as per ready reckoner value and then pay the same as per schedule fixed by the authority.

Relaxation on Road development:

As per the new DCR under a cluster redevelopment, having two roads is mandatory, and the road's width should be sufficient to load TRD, FSI, etc.

If the co-operating housing societies are willing to go for cluster self-redevelopment, two road requirement would be relaxed with regards to the open space requirement.

Appointment of contractor:

CHS has to appoint a contractor to carry out the redevelopment of the building. Society has to choose contractors from the list maintained by the planning authority. The contractor has to submit balance sheets for the last three years. This requirement will ensure that the average or any tom, dick and harry can't get the work of redevelopment. The contractor can be debarred from work if the committee monitoring the project finds that it is being delayed due to the contractor. That contractor will be blacklisted and would not be allowed to take self-redevelopment in future. This step will ensure the work is carried on time with a proper schedule.

Concession in Stamp duty:

Under this scheme, existing society members will not be liable for stamp duty for the flat allotted to them in the new building. If the existing member opts to buy a new flat under Prime Minister Awas Yojana (PMAY), the stamp duty will be Rs 1000 only per flat. And if the member opts for a larger area other than applicable, the same cap of Rs 1000 is applicable. Stamp duty should be paid for other flats sold in an open market as per the ready reckoner rates.

Subsidy for construction loan

If the CHS applies for a construction loan under GR, it shall get a subsidy of 4% per annum interest rate. As per Mumbai Bank's policy for self-redevelopment, the interest rate is 12.5% per annum, which will reduce it to 8.50% per annum. To give the lender bank a say in the redevelopment, the loan agreement should be a tripartite agreement between the Cooperative Housing Society (CHS), lender bank and the contractor. The lender will also be eligible to appoint at least one member in the three members' committee. All the construction conditions are to be mentioned in the agreement; including the release of funds. In addition, the lender bank can also assess the contractor's financial capacity.

Vigilance committee:

The self-redevelopment process should be transparent, controlled and monitored precisely; if there is an issue, it should be addressed. To overcome all the challenges and issue, every CHS opting for self-redevelopment has to form a vigilance committee as per government directive. The concerned CHS shall form a vigilance committee for supervising and controlling the development process, with at least two representatives from the society and a minimum of one representative from a financial institution. The vigilance committee must submit a progress report to the CHS and the planning authority every three months. The CHS and the financial institute may further define the scope of the committee.

Grievance redressal committee:

In case dispute/complaints or objection arises between various stakeholders. The Government had formed a grievance redressal committee on every district level. This committee will include the following officers.

- District Dy. Registrar in the concerned district or representative nominated by him.

- Officer authorised by the planning authority in the concerned district.

- Any complaints regarding self-redevelopment should be addressed to such district-level grievances committee.

Chapter 8

Analysis of the Government Resolution on Self- Redevelopment

On September 13 2019, the Maharashtra State issued a Government Resolution (GR) outlining rules for societies undertaking self-redevelopment. The GR states that any building over 30 years old can initiate the process of self-redevelopment.

Maharashtra state government is offering various incentives and concessions to help housing societies carry out the self-redevelopment of their old buildings.

This move by the Government of Maharashtra will bring about simplicity in the redevelopment process and will induce confidence among residents as they can plan for their societies.

The same authorities currently approving the redevelopment of housing societies in the state will be the planning authority for the self-development of the cooperative housing societies.

The key highlights of this Government Resolution are as follows:

- There would be a one-window system for all permissions.

- Faster and time-bound approvals as plans will be approved within six months from the date of submission.

- 10% Extra floor space index (FSI).

- Plots abutting road width less than 9 meters will be allowed 0.4 FSI free of cost.

- Societies will get concessions in the purchase of TDR (50% concession).

- Societies will also get concessions on premiums payable;

- Societies will get Installments in premiums payable to Municipal Corporation and don't have to pay all premiums upfront.

- Rebates on loans of 4%;

- Penalising erring contractors who delay construction work;

- Reduction in Land Under Construction Cost;

- Reduction in Goods & Service Tax (GST)

- 1000/- Stamp Duty only for Permanent Alternate Accommodation Agreement (PAAA)

- To protect residents from delays, the Government has also mandated that the project needs to be completed within three years after approvals are issued.

- There will be a tri-partite agreement between the Housing Society, the Banks Disbursing loans and the Contractor.

- The state has also announced a vigilance committee to ensure quality construction and monitor its time frame.

- There will be a grievance redressal cell to protect the residents and a mechanism to remove erring contractors and blacklist their firms.

A deep analysis of this government resolution points out the following:

- One window clearing system is a welcome move, removing many hurdles for society and making it easier for them to approach just one authority\

- Time-bound approval of a maximum of six months will help in starting the project on time.

- Extra FSI, concession on purchase of TDR, and Flat rate of stamp duty will all entice the members of cooperative housing society to go in for Self-redevelopment

- Concession in interest in case of bank loan will further help the society in saving costs of construction.

The GR issued by the Government is comprehensive and does try to address the major problems faced by the members when it comes to Builder led the development

With this much-needed GR for Mumbai, more and more Housing Societies will look for going in for Self-redevelopment as the Government has given good regulatory support and a much-needed push in the right direction, which will further result in the making of an ecosystem in this regard.

Chapter 9

Importance of Self-redevelopment

For residents of many older housing communities, going to rebuild their community can be a daunting task. The builders are notorious for delaying the project and stretching it over a long period of time, leaving homeowners homeless. Tired of such tall promises and long delays by the builders, housing communities are increasingly choosing Self Redevelopment. Here, residents keep builders out of the equation and instead appoint a contractor and project management coordinator to help carry out the project. The practice has collected smoke in Mumbai, where 750 unusual communities have chosen to improve themselves.

Should your housing community also consider it?

Taking back control:

Builders found reconstruction projects attractive as there is an excellent opportunity to profit by selling additional flats/inventory left after giving flats/units to the original members. The builder gets to pocket all the profits from the easy-to-sell market. However, under a self-development project, any surplus acquired in the sale of additional assets is retained entirely by the society to be shared equally among its members.

The major advantage of self-redevelopment is that society members reap the benefits of the unused potential of the property rather than the builder

Alternatively, the public members can expect to get around 40-50% more carpet area than their current dwellings compared to the 15-20% promised by the builders. The community also maintains control over all aspects of development. It can determine the type of facilities - parking, pool, children's play area, etc. - which will be included in the project and set aside the selection of new members in the market. While the builder assumes the immutable power of attorney (POA) to the members, when the land rights are handed over to him, all property rights remain with the community in the event of redevelopment.

Why does Mumbai need Self-Redevelopment?

Most residential buildings in Mumbai have been around for decades. Some of these structures may be restored and given a few more years of life, while others are not. Reconstruction is the only option in all of these buildings.

Many residents had purchased apartments when they had a small family. As the second generation grows and expands families, the flats' size becomes a challenge to deal with. And with rising rental costs and new apartments, choosing to rebuild becomes a much more practical option.

In the 60s, most buildings in Mumbai were built by members of the community itself. They will come together, build a community, raise funds through donations and mortgages, put projects in place, and select contractors to build the building. These structures are constructed according to the members' needs and quality standards. Later, when the procedures started to become complicated and a tedious process, the communities, started to get out of the way, and builders entered the scene.

Often many communities prefer to renovate their buildings with Real Estate engineers as they do not know all the requirements. Reconstruction through Real Estate Developers is a debate in which both parties strive to achieve the highest possible benefits. These conflicts often lead to situations and consequences that do not suit members of the community. When it comes to reconstruction through Building Developers, there have been several issues raised in the past, such as the following:-

- Careless management of all work

- Allegations of corruption and smuggling

- Developers changing building plans in their favour without informing community members

- Developers trying to grab and sell common areas

- Financial mismanagement - Money raised/received from the current project is used to finance other projects, which leads to cash flow issues and sometimes also results in the stagnancy of the projects

According to media reports, more than 5800 projects are currently under construction in Mumbai, affecting more than 1,25,000 families. There are many reasons why all these projects are stuck. They range from budget shortages to permit delays to incorrect calculations in the area allocated.

For members of the society, taking on their housing community's self-improvement keeps members safe from the builder's problems. The community is assured of additional benefits and profits from the project. This is possible as the overall management of the project remains in the hands of the public.

To make the development process in Mumbai easier for housing communities, there are Project Managers who provide professional management services in relation to development projects in Mumbai.

Also, authorities have begun taking steps to promote Mumbai's self-development by establishing the Self Redevelopment Scheme for

Mumbai through a dedicated single-window program established by MHADA to enable rapid approval of self-development projects.

Mumbai District Central Co-operative Bank Ltd (MDCC Bank / Mumbai Bank) is authorised to finance development projects in Mumbai and provides up to 95% of project costs.

When done correctly, the self-redevelopment projects in Mumbai can completely change the pace of development in Mumbai and help solve the city's acute housing shortage in the long run.

Self-improvement in Mumbai has many benefits and is quickly being recognised among housing communities in Mumbai. By choosing Self Development in Mumbai, communities can access development finance loans and select supervisors and contractors who will work according to their needs. This effectively cuts the builder out of the process. It also ensures that the process is transparent and safe with additional control in the hands of the society to oversee the creation of a better-quality result.

Old Structures of Mumbai:

Large Number of Nuclear Families:

Benefits of Self-Redevelopment

In this chapter we will understand the benefits of Self Redevelopment, they are enumerated below

Benefits:

- All profits from a marketable property go to the community, not to the developer.

- Higher carpet space of up to 50-60% is given to the existing members compared to 10-15% given by a builder.

- As resources are determined by members; they are expected to make the most optimum use of it and reduce the wastages, if any

- Existing ones select the new members.

- All property rights reside with the community

- No member of the public should mortgage his or her apartment at the Bank.

- Complete control in the hands of the Members of the Association

- In the development process, community members have the power to manage a project where they can decide on plans, construction and set development standards. Members of the society can, therefore, determine even the quality of construction.

- Community members can also decide on the services they want to have in the developed community, such as parking lots, children's playgrounds etc.

- Also, building plans cannot be changed without the consent of members.

Chapter 11

Responsibility of Society

The society should discuss and develop an internal redevelopment team amongst the members themselves to see whether the work is going on at a good pace and no fraudulent activities occur in the redevelopment process.

Responsibilities are then to be assigned to the Redevelopment team members who are chosen from among the society members themselves, considering their expertise and availability of time. The appointment of Experienced and well know consultants should be done in a transparent manner and that which provides the maximum benefits. Society should prepare proper, exhaustive and legally binding contract documents to avoid any legal complications in the future.

Society should also prepare to raise some funds as per the required cash flow statement. Sale flats will have to be sold by the society, which will provide revenue and cover costs of construction and other costs. Society has to look upon end to end process, which includes but is not limited to finalising Marketing, Financial, Sales and Technical strategies, among others.

Society should be aware of certain essential norms and must be in compliance with all the laws applicable like RERA, GST, Income Tax, Maharashtra Cooperative Societies Act, 1960, Labour laws etc., for which it can hire consultants and understand the nitty-gritty of various laws which will have to be complied with

Line of Action to be followed by the society:

Appointment of Consultants:

Society is responsible for the appointment of Consultants for each activity. A Project Management Consultant, Architect, Contractor, Structural Consultant, Advocate/Legal Consultant, among others need to be appointed, which will help in the end to end activities from starting to finishing the self-redevelopment project.

Documentation & Survey:

Collecting the latest Land and Building documents and records, checking the Conveyance Deed and the Land Title status. Detailed contour survey of the society land's existing plot boundary. Understanding each flat's existing built-up area.

Project Report:

Scrutiny of Approved Plans and the current status of the building. Evaluate the available schemes for redevelopment & prepare a detailed area statement as per the Bye-Laws of Local Authorities. Preparation of project feasibility Report & Approval by SGBM.

Bank Loan Application:

The society, with the help of PMC, will prepare the files for submission of the loan application to The Mumbai District Central Co-operative Bank Ltd. (MDCC bank). The MDCC bank will verify the documents

& pre- sanction the loan amount. The Bank will provide 95% of the project cost.

Finalisation of Contractor:

A contractor will be finalised by society in the General Body Meeting, considering, among other eligibility conditions, the Capability, Credibility & Commercial Offer of the Contractor. The Contract Agreement will be signed by & between the society, the contractor & the Bank.

Submission and Approval of Plans:

The Architect will procure the Relevant NOCs & Fresh Documents. The Architect will submit the plans for approval to the Brihanmumbai Municipal Corporation. The respective Authorities will internally approve the plans & offer a Demand Note for the payment towards development charges, staircase premium, fungible premium, Fees & Deposits etc. The Demand Note received from BMC will be submitted to the MDCC bank. Based on the Principal Loan Approval, MDCC bank will release the payment to BMC against the demand note. The BMC will issue its Permit/ IOD/Approval of plans. Upon further compliance, BMC will issue its Commencement Certificate.

Shifting and Demolition:

Upon receipt of approval from BMC, the Individual flat Agreement is Signed & Registered by & between society & each society member. Upon handing over rent, brokerage & shifting charges, the society members will shift to temporary alternate accommodation and vacate the existing premises. The existing building will be demolished after the members have been relocated.

Construction Activity:

The Architect/PMC, Society Managing Committee & contractor will work out the Action Plan for Construction Activity. Some of the key decisions include:-

- Setting up of Labour Camp

- Society & Site Office

- Storage of Building Materials

- Schedule of construction activity (Bar Chart) etc.

Architect/ PMC & Structural Consultant will make Periodic & Quality of the construction work.

Repayment of Loan Amount:

Revenue received from the sale of flats in the open market shall be utilised to repay the interest & capital of the total amount. The Loan amount can be repaid during the construction period or after the successful completion of the self-redevelopment project. Formality towards closer of loan account will be performed by & between society & Bank.

Chapter 12

Financing Self Redevelopment

There are many ways to finance a Self-Development project, they are as follows:

Invite existing flat owners in society to buy free sale flats at a lower rate compared to the market rate:

The new flats are constructed for sale component with a discounted price, and society members who have initiated the self-redevelopment project can be convinced to invest in the new flats. This means they are charged construction cost + Profit (20% of the market selling price), which is a perfect opportunity for society to buy a flat at a lesser price than the market price. They can also benefit from the extra area at the concessional rate if the tenant wants to invest in their property. And these procedures help society to raise funds for the project.

Funding from Non-Banking Finance Companies (NBFC):

Up to 85% to 95% of the total project amount Government encourages banks to finance self-redevelopment projects, and Bank like Mumbai District Central Co-operative bank grant loan amounts, but banks sanction the loan for a self-redevelopment project after society clear Intimation of Disapproval or IOD from Government authorities.

Therefore, society has to bear the initial amount for the project, which is considered a total project cost of 15% on a large scale. Here, NBFC plays a vital and helpful role in finance the project in its initial stage up to IOD clearance. Against mortgage of land or any other valuable and ensured asset NBFC grant loan.

Inviting Investors to Invest in The Project:

To invest in property, society members can invite their friends and relatives who are interested. Also, to invest in real estate, society members can invite external investors interested. This work can also be done by brokers operating in the market or advertising the project using newspapers, banners, and digital marketing platforms like Facebook, Instagram, WhatsApp, etc.

Offers to encourage the investors can be made by making payment terms favorable to the investors. For example, payment terms 50% on application, and balance payment is completing work stages.

Bank Loan:

Banks are known as an essential source of finance, and in the case of self-redevelopment projects, banks play a vital role in financial aspects. To approve a loan for the self-redevelopment project is the essential requirement from the Bank where the building is located should be owned by a society which means have a conveyance deed in their name to get available finance approval from Bank.

Banks are particular about the conveyance deed of societies because Bank mortgage the land from society against the finance it provides to society.

Banks grant the loan amount of 85% to 95% of the total amount of the project and bank charges 12.5% of interest rate on loan amount annually. But a rebate of 4% is available under the scheme which brings down the effective interest rate to 8.5%

INR 50 crore is the maximum loan amount avail under the self-redevelopment scheme 2018.

Loan under this scheme is available for seven years and out of which two years is a moratorium period where no payment is required to be made to the Bank.

As per Government's new policy, Mumbai District Central Co-operative bank has been appointed as a nodal agency for financing self-redevelopment projects. Also, to boost and promote self-redevelopment project government provides an interest subsidy of 4% per annum.

Inviting deposits from society members:

Inviting existing society members to deposit their money against a lucrative return in the form of a 10% to 12% annual return rate. This way can adopt by passing a resolution in society meeting and with a definite guarantee of return.

Barter system:

Appointing Contractor on Barter System, whereby contractor gets right to sell few flats equivalent to its cost against the total cost of construction. The contractor can also fund the initial phase to pay charges to BMC before approval of plans. Society can also purchase TDR from its owner under the Barter system.

Chapter 13

Documents Needed

As any other development, even Self- Redevelopment process involves various documentations to be done, they are enlisted below

Society and its members:

- Society Registration Certificate with a copy of updated byelaws of the society
- Land ownership proof – Conveyance Deed or Index II or Sale Deed in the favor of the society or Land purchase agreement in the name of the society
- Original Building Plan, 6/12 extract, 7/12 extract and Property Card
- N. A. Order
- CTS Plan (or City Survey Plan) with CTS number
- Audited financial statements for last three financial years
- List of members and their current carpet areas as per plans
- List of managing committee
- Members share certificates and agreements.
- Setback area details
- Physical plot area measurements

Required by Bank (MDCC bank):

- Copy of Acknowledgement of the SGM Resolution

- Copy of the registration certificate and updated byelaws of the society. Audited financial statements for last three financial years

- List of committee members

- Details of all society members

- Copy of the proposed Self Redevelopment project report which should include details on the budget and cost break-up for the project

- Copies of IOD and other NOCs from concerned authorities etc.

- Existing Members Old and New Allotment with Existing Area, Free offer Area and Total Area Statement

- Amenities List proposed in the new Self Redevelopment project

- Copies of agreements entered into with the legal advisers, architects, chartered accountants etc. (the society has to shortlist and select them first)

- Cashflows of the project along with a loan repayment plan

  (Source: selfredevelopment.org)

Chapter 14

RBI & Self Re-Development Funding Policies

Reserve Bank of India has included Cooperative housing societies in the list of borrowers allowed to avail housing finance loans.

For the first time cooperative housing societies have been allowed to borrow from housing finance companies (HFCs). Earlier, societies in Mumbai could obtain loans for self-redevelopment only from the Mumbai District Central Co-operative Bank.

In a master direction issued by RBI in 2021 the RBI said, "Housing finance shall mean financing for purchase/construction/reconstruction/renovation/repairs of residential dwelling units which includes loans to individuals or groups of individuals including co-operative societies for construction/purchase of new dwelling units."

With this RBI opened doors for Housing finance companies to sanction loans to such societies going in for Self-Redevelopment, this move itself was expected to give boost to over 150 Housing Finance Companies (HFCs) registered with the RBI

RBI had earlier in 2020 circular restricted Cooperative banks from such types of transactions as they fell in the commercial real estate category, this meant Mumbai District Central Co-operative bank among other cooperatives were no longer able to sanction loans for such redevelopment projects

The move by RBI to restrict cooperative banks to extend loans for Self-Redevelopment project was not welcomed by many stakeholders.

RBI on 8th June 2022, issued a statement and a circular by which it allowed individual housing loans and Commercial Real Estate-Residential Housing funding by Cooperatives, District Central Cooperative Banks and State Cooperative Banks.

As such the earlier circular is now invalid and the cooperatives can again start lending for such Self Redevelopment projects.

This move is now expected to restore the credit, increase liquidity and financing avenues for Cooperative housing societies choosing to opt for Self-Redevelopment

Figure 27: RBI

Figure 28: RBI Headquarters in Mumbai

Challenges faced in Self-Redevelopment

While self-development is the best way to rebuild Mumbai, it's not as easy as a standard builder-led reconstruction. This is because, in the event of self-improvement, community members hae to take full responsibility of such development.

Before starting to improve, community members need to be aware of a few challenges they may face:

1) Decision making:

- Decision-making can be challenging with the diversity of views of community members.

- Finding consensus among members at the beginning and various stages of the project

2) Lack of legal and technical knowledge:

- Lack of technology or process knowledge

- Lack of knowledge of official documents

- Managing documents by government officials.

- Problems with understanding trends and managing TDR / FSI

3) Problems with Finance:

- Especially to receive IOD, since Financial Institutions fund only post receipt of IOD

4) Lack of accounting, human resource management and project management skills:

- Manage invoicing, tax and project cost calculations
- Maintaining a project construction tab in line with Government policies and best standards
- Managing multiple professionals from time to time and the necessary communication within them
- Time, skill and the tendency among community members to manage a significant self-improvement project
- Dealing with multiple authorities and experts
- Problems in understanding Network connectivity
- Lack of leadership and unity among community members

5) Lack of marketing skills:

- Ability to sell more flats to cover project costs.
- Disbursement of Financial, Construction and Renewal Costs.
- The community needs to deal with more departments.
- Time of Needs, Trends, Money and Power
- Requires "24 x 7 x 365" Professional Back-up.
- Not all members have the necessary knowledge or time to go to various agencies and appoint various advisers.

Chapter 16

Development Manager Model in Self-Redevelopment

In Development Management (DM) Model, Society also has liberty and freedom to allot their flats as per their wish, finalise all internal and external amenities as per their budget with the help of their appointed PMC Professional Team.

A Development Manager is a role which has more responsibilities than a PMC. A Development Manager is a more strategic team that envisages the entire project from maximising the success rate perspective while mitigating the risks. While the basic responsibilities of PMC are included in the scope of a Development Manager, there are further skills that a DM brings to the table.

In the DM model, instead of Mumbai District Central Cooperative Bank funding the loan, DM arranges a loan for the project. The role of Development Manager is not only to arrange uninterrupted funds for the project but also to look after Construction Management, Site Management, Sales Management, and Share their Brand & construction knowledge. All of this is done in exchange for fees.

Currently Development Managers are either Renowned Contractors or Developer firms who have a decent track record. Hence the project is professionally managed by the Society, PMC & DM.

There are few Developers who have a good track record and charge fixed margins. They are interested in executing the project because, in self redevelopment, all members are ready, and society is ready with plans, amenities list, and allotment of plans.

Chapter 17

Case Study: Mumbai District Central Cooperative Bank

Mumbai District Central Cooperative Bank, also known as Mumbai Bank, started giving out loans for self-development to Cooperative housing societies from 2017 onwards.

Commonly known as the Self Redevelopment Mumbai Bank, MDCCB or MDCC Bank is the only cooperative Bank in Mumbai currently providing loans for self-redevelopment projects in Mumbai.

The Bank funds up to 95% of the project cost at a simple rate of interest of 12.5% per year. The remaining 5% is required to be arranged by the society members. This 5% can be generated through society members purchasing extra areas or an additional unit in the redeveloped project or through external investors.

The Bank provides a loan repayment period of 7 years for projects up to Rs. 50 Crores. Out of these seven years, the first two years are the Moratorium period, during which the interest is accrued, but the society can pay the Bank after the period is over. The loan repayment period begins after the moratorium period. The total loan repayment period and moratorium period are extended to 10 years and three years, respectively, for projects more than Rs. 50 Crores.

At the end of the moratorium period, the interest accumulated has to be first cleared by the housing society. Once the interest is cleared, the installments towards repayment of the loan shall be determined by the Bank. The housing society can, however prepay the loan before the tenure for which there shall be no prepayment penalty.

MDCC Bank takes into consideration the cost of buying TDRs, fungible premium, cost of rent for alternate accommodation during the time the new building will be reconstructed, shifting and re-shifting of tenants, brokerage for sale of extra flats, professional fees to agencies, construction cost and other amenities planned like play area, garden etc. while considering the total project cost for a self-redevelopment project.

(Source: Taxguru)

Case Study: Success Stories

Jin Prem Housing Society:

Located at Charkop in Mumbai, it claims to be the first such self-redevelopment society in greater Mumbai. For the project, no funds were borrowed from any financial institution and all the planning, funding, and other activities were done by 28 members of the society, all of whom have shifted to their new homes. The new development is a 14 story building having 53 flats, each being a 3bhk flat of about 705 sq ft carpet space.

Figure 29: Jin Prem Housing Society

New Tilak Nagar Riddhi Siddhi CHS:

Located in chembur, the society is spread across 998 sq mtr plot, the plot belonged to MHADA, had 40 members, currently the self-redevelopment process is underway.

Mukund Employee's CHS:

Located in Govind Nagar in Ghatkopar West is a society spread across 2,068 sq mtr. 43 members of the society came together to go in for self redevelopment, currently the self-redevelopment process is underway

Om Rameshwar CHS:

Located in Borivali East, 26 members of the society came together, currently the self-redevelopment process is underway

Malad Apartment CHSL:

Located in Malad west, 45 members of the society have come together for the development, the society is spread across 2,193 sq mtr of plot area; currently the self-redevelopment process is underway

Chitra Cooperative Housing Society:

Located in Shahakar Nagar, chembur is a planned 15 story building out of which 12 have been completed. The 12 original members will get flats almost double their old tenantments of 450 sq ft, additionally 32 flats will be sold in the open market.

Purvarang Society:

Located in Mulund, is a planned 23 story building out of which six floors have been constructed. 56 members of the society came together and will get double their old tenantments of around 425 sq ft. the building will now have 118 flats in total

Shalimar Society:

Located in charkop, members have vacated the building after getting all approvals, work will start soon.

Kshitij Society:

Located in charkop, pilling work has been completed, and construction is progressing at a good speed.

Shwetambara Society:

Located in Charkop, work is going on in full swing, with over six floors already being constructed.

Abhilasha Society:

Located in Charkop, the society has received preliminary permissions for the self-redevelopment of the society.

Others:

- Tillibai CHS in Malad
- 6 Societies in Shailendra Nagar in Dahisar
- Ekta Society in Girgaum
- Amit Xavier CHS

- Ganesh Baug CHS

- Hari Om Sai Sadan CHS

- Sagar Sameer CHS

- Rajendra Nagar Vikas CHS

- Abhilasha CHSL

- Malad Sati Darshan CHSL

- Sailesh Vihar CHSL

- Manusmruti CHSL

- Sea Rock CHS

- Dinnaco Darshan CHS

(Source: Toughconsnirman, WeDevelopment, Mumbai Mirror)

SBUT - An Unique Initiative in Cluster Re-Development

Saifee Burhani Upliftment Trust (SBUT) is a non-profit organisation engaged and undertaking the development of the Bhendi Bazaar cluster development. This project is one of India's largest makeover project as it impacts around 20,000 people.

The project spans over an area of 16.5 acres comprising 250 decrepit buildings, 3,200 families, and 1,250 shops. It is transforming into a modern and elaborate sustainable development embodying 11 new towers, wider roads, modern infrastructure, open spaces, and commercial areas, among others.

In 2019, the first phase of the project was completed with the construction of the high-rise Al Sa'adah Towers. During rehabilitation at Bhendi Bazaar, the first 610 families returned to the towers as owners of the new residential flats in 2020. These towers also encompass 128 commercial shop owners who have been provided state-of-the-art infrastructure.

As of February 2021, after completing the Phase 1 work of the Bhendi Bazar redevelopment project, the SBUT has initiated the Phase 2 construction work.

Bhendi Bazaar redevelopment is one of the most complex type of redevelopment project being undertaken due to the number of tenants, structures/buildings to be redeveloped.

This project is one of the first large redevelopment projects being executed under the state government's cluster redevelopment policy announced in 2009 reportedly. It is being executed by Saifee Burhani Upliftment Trust (SBUT), which is a trust formed by Dawoodi Bohra Community members who were the main occupiers of these buildings to be redeveloped.

Figure 30: Bhendi Bazaar in Mumbai

Figure 31: Proposed Redevelopment Plan for Bhendi Bazaar

As of February 2024, the construction is at an advance stage. Phase 2 is currently under construction. In Sector 6, Two towers of 53 floors each will replace 23 old and dilapidated buildings on a plot of approximately 1.34 acres. It will house more than 1,250 families and around 270 shops

In sector 4, Two towers of 53 floors each will replace 74 old and dilapidated buildings on a plot of approximately 1.5 acres. It will house more than 1,350 families and around 320 shops

The project is ongoing successfully and in all probability will finish successfully and showcase a case study for the world to see and marvel at.

Self Redevelopment in 2024

In 2023, In order to ease the self-redevelopment of old buildings in Maharashtra, especially in Mumbai, the Maharashtra government has set the ball rolling by instructing authorities to approve proposals for self-redevelopment within three months.

The direction was given by the Maharashtra Housing Department by way of a government resolution (GR) dated August 29, 2023.

In April, 2024, Maharashtra States first self-redevelopment without a loan facility was completed after a 7 year timeline and gestation. The project- **Purvarang Cooperative Housing Society** in eastern suburbs of Mumbai, having around 56 families was successfully completed. The 23 storey tower was built without any loan facility.

The families earlier occupied house of 390 sq. ft. abut after self-redevelopment the same families will now be owners of a spacious 3 BHK apartment of 1,015 sq. ft

In 2023 and as recently as few months ago too, many buildings were in different stages of self-redevelopment, few of them are as follows:

- Shwetambara society in Charkop

- Kshitij society in Charkop

- Shalimar society in Charkop

- Abhilasha society

- Tillibai society in Malad

- Rang Tarang Society in Dahisar

- Good Earth society in Chembur

- Kesar Kripa Society in Borivali

- Swayambhu society in Akurli

- Sarjivan society in Malad

Many such societies across Mumbai Metropolitan Region have chosen to go under this route. The response received since last few years has been impressive with many more societies choosing to go under this model of redevelopment. The response has been disproportionately high in suburbs of Mumbai.

NATIONAL BEST SELLING REAL ESTATE SERIES